Veggie Food
for Kids

hamlyn

Veggie Food for Kids

Sara Lewis

This book is dedicated to my children Alice and William

First published in Great Britain in 2001 by Hamlyn
a division of Octopus Publishing Group Limited
2–4 Heron Quays
London E14 4JP

First published in paperback in 2003

ISBN 0 600 608875

British Library Cataloguing-in-Publication Data
A catalogue record for this book is available from the British Library

Printed and bound in China
10 9 8 7 6 5 4 3 2 1

NOTES

Standard level spoon measures are used in all recipes
1 tablespoon = one 15 ml spoon
1 teaspoon = one 5 ml spoon

Both metric and imperial measurements are given for the recipes. Use one set of measures only, not a mixture of both.

Ovens should be preheated to the specified temperature. If using a fan-assisted oven, follow the manufacturer's instructions for adjusting the time and temperature. Grills should also be preheated.

Free-range medium eggs should be used unless otherwise stated.

Use full-fat milk unless otherwise specified.

Pepper should be freshly ground unless otherwise specified.

Ideally stock should be freshly made; see recipe on page 38. Alternatively, buy a carton of fresh stock, ensuring it is salt-free for under-ones.

Buy cheese labelled with the vegetarian symbol to ensure it is made with vegetarian rennet.

A few recipes include nuts and nut derivatives. Anyone with a known nut allergy must avoid these. Children under the age of 3 with a family history of nut allergy, asthma, eczema or any other type of allergy are also advised to avoid eating dishes which contain nuts. Do not give whole nuts or seeds to any child under 5 because of the risk of choking.

Contents

introduction

It is no longer considered cranky and eccentric to be a vegetarian. There are no less than 4 million vegetarians in this country and this number is increasing, by approximately 5,000 each week. It isn't only vegetarians who enjoy meat-free meals – a staggering 10 million people in the UK no longer eat red meat and vegetarian meals feature strongly in their diet.

A well-balanced vegetarian diet provides all of the nutrients needed for good health. Research also suggests that a vegetarian diet is better in the long term too – statistically, vegetarians are 30% less likely to suffer heart disease, 40% less likely to get cancer, and are less prone to diet-related diabetes, obesity, kidney disease, gallstones and high blood pressure too. Certain potentially fatal diseases, such as CJD and E-coli food poisoning, are avoided if you are vegetarian.

Most of us who adopt a meat-free diet are opposed to animal cruelty – some 800 million animals are slaughtered each year in the UK alone – but many people are unaware of the detrimental effect that intense cattle production and fishing has on our land and seas. It can take up to 10 kilos of vegetable protein and 100,000 litres of water to produce just 1 kg of meat, while it takes just 900 litres of water to grow 1 kg of wheat. So a vegetarian diet is more environmentally friendly too.

As parents we all want to do the best for our children and that includes the foods we offer them. These are vital, not simply to show them how much we care, but for their growth and well being too. Just as there are critical periods for learning to walk, speak and recognise people, there seems to be a critical period for the development of taste preferences.

The foundations for adult food preferences are laid during a child's first two years and many children find it hard to accept types of food that are not offered during those crucial early years. 'Nursery food' will always have certain appeal to young children but it is most important to offer your child an interesting and varied diet based on plenty of fruit and vegetables, mixed grains and protein from milk and dairy products, eggs, pulses, nuts and seeds, and soya-rich products.

This book is packed with practical and helpful advice on feeding a vegetarian family, plus easy everyday recipes your children will love. It is aimed at those families new to the joys of a meat-free lifestyle, and to vegetarian couples as they approach parenthood. I hope it will also prove a source of inspiration to long-established vegetarian families. Many dishes include dairy products and eggs, but those who wish to follow a stricter dairy-free diet will find suitable vegan recipes and helpful advice too.

By keeping meat off the menu, we will bring up the next generation as vegetarians who eat well, stay healthy and care for our environment. What better and more positive lesson can there be to teach our children?

FEEDING YOUR BABY

Decide on a vegetarian diet for your baby and you may meet with some scepticism or disapproval, even today. Don't be discouraged by others – the British Medical Association now recognises that a vegetarian diet can provide all of the nutrients a growing infant needs. Indeed all babies follow a vegetarian diet for the first few weeks of their lives.

BABY'S FIRST FOOD: MILK

In the early months, the only food that a baby requires to meet all of his or her nutritional needs is milk – either breast milk or formula. All babies are born with a store of iron to last for the first 6 months and this is supplemented, to an extent, by the milk too.

Breast milk gives your baby the best start in life and is the ideal food and drink. It contains all the nutrients your baby needs in the right proportions, as well as many antibodies which help fight infections. The high levels of fatty acids also protect a baby susceptible to allergies. Iron levels are low in breast milk but they are in a readily absorbed form and combine with your baby's own iron store to meet his or her requirements for the first 6 months.

Breast milk can also adjust if your baby is premature, alter as your baby grows and his needs change, and even dilute in hot weather to satisfy a baby's thirst. Breastfeeding is sterile, free, and always ready at the right temperature, virtually on demand.

Breastfeeding, like any new skill, can be difficult especially in the early days. Do persevere if you can and don't be afraid to seek advice from your midwife, health visitor or breastfeeding counsellor. Continue until your baby is 6 weeks, 6 months or 1 year old, or until you and your baby are ready to stop. If you want to bring your baby up following a vegan diet, try to breastfeed up to 12 months, offering morning and night feeds from 6 months, before going on to soya infant formula.

FORMULA MILK

Formulas are powdered cow's milk especially modified to be as close to the nutritional composition of breast milk as possible and fortified with vitamins and minerals. Whey-based formulas are given to newborn babies. Follow-on formulas have a higher proportion of casein to whey, and are suited to hungrier babies over 6 months. Make up formula feeds with previously boiled water and refrigerate until required. Avoid the use of repeatedly boiled water, softened water or bottled water which can be high in some mineral salts. Continue with formula milk feeds until your baby is 12 months, then progress to full-fat cow's milk.

SOYA BASED INFANT FORMULA

You may want to include this formula in your baby's diet if you follow a dairy-free diet, or if your baby develops a lactose intolerance. Regardless of the reason, you must seek medical advice before going on to soya milk. Your doctor may prescribe this formula free of charge on prescription.

Unlike other milks, soya does not contain sugar and is often sweetened with glucose syrup, which can be detrimental to teeth. Some soya formulas also contain small levels of aluminium and so are unsuitable for premature babies or those suffering kidney problems. Do not give babies unmodified (or carton) soya milks before they are 2 years old.

GOAT'S MILK

Goat's milk infant formula is suitable from birth and can be less allergenic than cow's milk formula as it is more easily digested. Some babies who are sensitive to cow's milk formula may be able to tolerate goat's milk infant formula as it doesn't contain the gamma-casein present in cow's milk. Ask your health visitor about 'Nanny' infant formula. Do not give full-fat fresh goat's milk as a main drink to babies under 12 months.

COW'S MILK

Cow's milk is a good source of energy, protein, vitamins and minerals and is especially important for calcium, which is essential for growing teeth and bones. It should not be given as a drink to babies until 12 months, but can be added to cooking from 6 months.

FIRST SOLID FOODS

Most babies are ready to try their first few mini mouthfuls of solid food at around 4 months. At this stage you may notice that your baby doesn't seem fully satisfied after a feed, or seems generally restless and grizzly, or wakes up hungry more often in the night..

Don't be tempted to introduce solid foods before 4 months as your baby's digestive system will be too immature. You might also increase the likelihood of allergic reactions if you do so. For this reason, you may be advised to wait until nearer 6 months if you have a family history of allergy. New mothers often feel pressurized into offering their baby solid foods early on – simply because all their friends have. Don't yield to such pressure; it isn't a competition and there are advantages to waiting. Be guided by how you and your baby feel.

In the early days of weaning, the aim is to introduce your baby to the tastes and textures of foods other than milk, not for these new foods to provide lots of extra nourishment.

SITTING COMFORTABLY

At first you and your baby will probably feel happiest if he or she sits on your lap so that they feel secure. Protect your baby's clothes with a bib or muslin and your own with a tea towel. As feeding progresses and your baby grows, a baby's car seat – placed on a secure surface or the floor – may be easier.

Allow plenty of time so that you and your baby can enjoy this new experience. If you have older children, offer solids when your baby wakes after a mid-morning sleep when the other children are at school and the house is peaceful. You may prefer to give your baby a small milk feed first, then offer solid foods to follow.

INTRODUCING SOLIDS

Bought powdered baby rice is probably the easiest first food to offer as it is simple to prepare. Alternatively, you could offer finely puréed and sieved boiled potato. To prepare baby rice, mix 1 teaspoon of 'pure' baby rice to a smooth, slightly slopping consistency with breast milk or formula, or previously boiled and cooled water (see pack instructions). Offer this to your baby from a small rounded plastic baby spoon. The taste won't be too dissimilar to the milk your baby is used to, and should be happily received. If he or she appears distressed, stop and try

again in a few weeks' time.

Learning to take food off a spoon is a new skill and may take a while for your baby to grasp. Don't worry if more of the food dribbles out of the mouth than is consumed. At this stage your baby is learning to chew rather than just suck, and is still receiving all of his nutritional needs from milk.

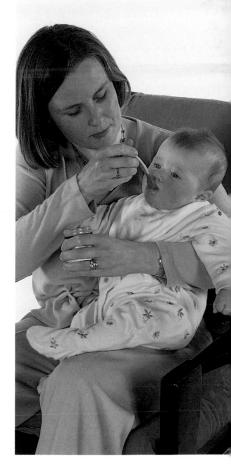

If your baby liked the rice, offer this again just once or twice during the next few days to allow time for his digestive system to adapt to 'solids'. If your baby seems to enjoy these first few mini mouthfuls, then move on and try:

• Puréed and sieved potato, sweet potato, butternut squash, parsnip or carrot. Peel and dice the vegetable, then steam until tender and purée with formula or breast milk, or boiled water. Or cook in a little water and formula or breast milk, then purée with this liquid.

• Puréed and sieved fruits, such as ripe banana, or cooked dessert apple or pear. Peel, core and slice the apple or pear and cook with a little boiled water but no sugar, then purée.

• Thin porridge of rice, corn meal (maize), sago or millet, mixed with formula or breast milk or boiled water.

At this stage, fruit and vegetable purées should be sieved to ensure they are completely smooth.

If your baby takes to solids readily, slowly build up to 2 mini meals each day over the next month to 6 weeks, adapting the amounts to suit your baby's appetite. Your baby should still be having breast milk or a minimum of 600 ml (1 pint) formula milk a day. Do not give wheat, oats, cow's or goat's milk, nuts, seeds or eggs at this stage.

BASIC EQUIPMENT

A variety of equipment can be used to make purées. A basic fork is all you need to mash potatoes and bananas. A nylon sieve is useful for puréeing small quantities of vegetables and fruit, while a hand operated mouli grater is ideal for slightly larger

quantities. An electric blender or food mill makes light work of puréeing, but does take a little longer to wash up. A food processor is less efficient, unless you are making baby food in bulk or have a mini bowl as an optional attachment.

You will need to sterilize bottles, teats and caps after each use, but it is no longer thought necessary to sterilize other items. Just make sure that everything needed to prepare and serve your baby's food is thoroughly clean.

Foods to avoid

• Salt – a baby's digestive system cannot cope with salty foods. Do not add salt when cooking for under-ones.

• Sugar – this could encourage a sweet tooth and lead to bad habits and tooth decay later on. Mix naturally sweet fruits with sharper ones in place of sugar. Do not add sugar when cooking for under-ones.

• Honey – don't give this to children under 1 year as it is high in sugar. Also, there is a small risk of food poisoning from unpasteurized honey.

• Nuts – do not give whole nuts to children under 5 because of the risk of choking. If there is a family history of peanut or other allergy, avoid nuts in any form until your child is 3 years old. Otherwise finely ground nuts (and seeds) may be offered from around 9–12 months. Seek advice from your health visitor or doctor if you are unsure. (See also Food Allergies, page 16.)

All change

Previously, health professionals advocated a slow introduction to new tastes, recommending that each new food be offered for several meals before introducing another. It is now thought better practice to introduce your baby to new flavours more quickly unless there is a family history of food allergies. Again, be guided by your child – some babies are quite adventurous, others find many different tastes off-putting and need to take things more slowly.

5–6 MONTHS

If you are introducing solids for the first time at this stage, follow the previous guidelines (see page 9). If your baby is already taking solids, gradually increase their frequency to 3 mini meals each day and try to space these evenly throughout the day. Build on the flavours your baby already enjoys and introduce simple combinations, such as carrot and cauliflower, and pear or apricot and rice. It is no longer essential to sieve all purées, but food still needs to be finely puréed.

Red lentils, simmered in boiled water and finely mashed or puréed with a little vegetable oil, can now be introduced. You can also offer your baby a wider variety of fruit and vegetables, including avocado, papaya and green vegetables. Avocado flesh is best mashed just before serving as it discolours quickly. Papaya is a lovely treat for your baby – halve and scrape away all of the tiny black seeds before puréeing. Because green vegetables have a more pronounced flavour, they are best mixed with a bland vegetable that your baby has tried and liked before, such as potato or butternut squash. Alternatively, mix with powdered rice.

Be guided by your baby's preferences and don't hurry him or her. Adjust the amount of food according to his appetite and don't try to persuade him to finish off that last spoonful – he will show you when he's had enough. Avoid bombarding your baby with too many new tastes in quick succession or you may put him off the idea of solids altogether. Instead, aim to increase your baby's repertoire of foods gradually. Maintain regular milk feeds, and never add sloppy baby foods to a baby's bottle. Keep wheat, oats, cow's and goat's milk, nuts and eggs off the menu.

6–9 MONTHS

At this stage, most babies will be munching their way through 3 mini meals a day, and weaning foods play a more important nutritional role. Your baby's natural store of iron will now be exhausted so it is important to include sufficient iron in their diet. Dark green vegetables, puréed and sieved cooked dried apricots, and small amounts of prune juice are suitable sources. Tiny amounts of fibrous pulses and lentils can also be introduced – boost the absorption of the iron these foods contain by serving with vitamin C-rich foods such as broccoli, a teaspoon of fresh orange juice, or by following with a fruity dessert.

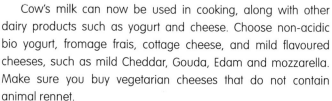

You can now start to introduce grains which contain gluten, including wheat, oats and barley, in the form of pasta, bread etc. Buy iron-fortified baby breakfast cereals for an added nutritional boost. Small amounts of tofu and hard-boiled egg yolk may be given too.

Cow's milk can now be used in cooking, along with other dairy products such as yogurt and cheese. Choose non-acidic bio yogurt, fromage frais, cottage cheese, and mild flavoured cheeses, such as mild Cheddar, Gouda, Edam and mozzarella. Make sure you buy vegetarian cheeses that do not contain animal rennet.

Although breast or formula milk feeds are still vitally important, you may find that your baby is happy to lose a lunchtime milk feed, in which case offer a drink of cooled, boiled water instead. Up to 8 months, milk is still your baby's main source of protein.

If you have a family history of allergies, then you may be advised to avoid giving your baby dairy products and eggs until 12 months, and to avoid nuts until a child is 3 years. (See also Food Allergies, page 16.)

From 6 to 12 months your baby will need between 700–1000 calories a day, compared to a mother's requirement of 2,000–2,500 calories. As baby appetites are small and growth rate high, it is important to give foods that are a concentrated source of nutrients, avoiding those that provide too much bulk. Use fibre-rich foods – such as beans and lentils – sparingly, and do not add refined bran. Avoid fresh or frozen green peas and dried chickpeas.

Each day, aim to offer a 6–9 month baby:
• 2 mini servings of vegetables and fruit
• 2 or 3 mini servings of starchy foods, such as potatoes, rice or unsweetened breakfast cereal
• 1 mini serving of protein-rich food, such as cheese, egg, tofu, beans or lentils.

Introducing a beaker
Introduce your baby to a lidded feeder beaker from around 6 months. Offer a little boiled and cooled water in it, when your baby has a lunchtime solid feed. If he isn't too keen, then try with a little formula or breast milk. If your baby is used to a bottle, comfort sucking can be a hard habit to break so try to encourage your baby to use a beaker and alternate between a bottle and beaker. Aim to wean your baby off a bottle by the time he is around 12 months. Avoid giving fruit juices, even unsweetened ones, to a baby in a bottle as the prolonged sucking on juice can result in tooth decay. Offer juices in a beaker at meal times. Resist the temptation to give a fractious baby a bottle to drink when out in the pushchair unless it is filled with water.

9–12 MONTHS

By now your baby may be happy to progress to slightly lumpier food but, as before, be guided by him or her. Some hate lumps of any kind and almost seem to gag on them. The most important thing at this stage is to offer variety. If the diet is very limited now, then it can be difficult to encourage children to try new foods later on.

Now that your baby's digestive system is able to cope with a little fibre, small portions of well cooked and mashed fresh or frozen peas, dried split peas and chickpeas may be offered. As long as allergy isn't a consideration, finely ground nuts, and smooth nut and seed butters can be introduced – add these to fruit and vegetable purées to boost protein levels. When you have time, make your own nut and seed butters (see pages 18 and 45).

Encourage your baby towards eating the same food as the rest of the family but make sure there are no added salt, sugar or hot spices.

Each day, aim to offer a 9–12 month baby:
• 3–4 mini servings of fruit and vegetables
• 3–4 mini servings of starchy foods
• 2 mini servings of protein-rich foods, such as eggs, cheese, tofu, lentils and beans.

FINGER FOODS

As your child's hand-eye co-ordination develops so their independence grows, and many young children are soon keen to feed themselves. Try not to worry about the mess. A spoon will

still be far too tricky to use effectively, so offer some foods that will be easy for your baby to hold:
• Broccoli or cauliflower florets, cooked until just tender
• Cooked carrot sticks
• Halved, sliced or mini bananas

Moving on to:
• peeled apple slices
• thickly sliced, peeled cucumber
• cubes of mild Cheddar
• raisins and sultanas (don't be alarmed if they seem to pass through almost whole!)
• toast fingers, strips of pitta bread, bread sticks, rice cakes. (Avoid Granary or multigrain bread as your baby could choke on the grains.)

Who needs water?

Very young breastfed babies do not need water because the composition of breast milk changes in hot weather to quench a baby's thirst. However, many are receptive to water if offered it from a bottle early on, and introducing a bottle can be helpful should you decide to change from breast to bottle feeding later on. A formula fed baby may need some water occasionally.

As weaning progresses, so the amount of milk your baby takes gradually reduces. If you decide to cut out a lunchtime milk feed altogether, then offer a small bottle or lidded feeder beaker with a little pure water.

Bottled still water that is low in minerals can be given – ask your health visitor about suitable brands. Sparkling mineral water isn't suitable.

If you use tap water, filter it and change the filter regularly to remove pollutants and chemicals. Or boil the water first, then leave to cool in a covered container. Only offer water that has been boiled once, as repetitive boiling concentrates natural salts present. Do not give your baby water from a tap fitted with a water-softening device.

Try to avoid sweetened baby juices, fortified with vitamin C. Encourage your child to drink more water and, rather than give fruit juice, include fruit in meals.

WHICH FOODS TO INTRODUCE AND WHEN

	4–5 MONTHS	5–6 MONTHS	6–9 MONTHS	9–12 MONTHS
VEGETABLES	Cooked, puréed and sieved potato, butternut squash, parsnip, carrot, sweet potato	Cooked and puréed mild green vegetables, such as cauliflower, courgettes and broccoli; mushrooms, celery	Stronger-tasting vegetables, such as spinach, cabbage, green beans, leek, onion; peppers, tiny amounts of tomato	Cooked broccoli, cauliflower and carrots as finger foods; well cooked mashed green peas
FRUIT	Puréed and sieved ripe banana; or apple or pear cooked with water but no sugar	Puréed avocado, papaya, melon; cooked fresh apricots and plums (sieved to remove skins)	Vitamin C-rich fruits, such as kiwi, mango, peach, a little citrus fruit such as orange; small quantities of dried apricots, dates, figs	Citrus fruits, strawberries and other berry fruits. Unsweetened fruit juices diluted 1 to 10 parts with cooled, boiled water
GRAINS, PULSES ETC	Baby rice, or cooked and puréed plain white rice; non-gluten grains, including cornmeal (polenta), millet; sago and tapioca	Cooked red lentils, puréed or finely mashed with a little vegetable oil	Wheat and other gluten cereals, such as pasta, barley, oats and plain flour in sauces. Small portions of well mashed beans and lentils	A wider range of grains, but limited unrefined grains. Introduce cooked dried peas in casseroles and homemade hummus
DAIRY FOODS AND TOFU	–	–	Cow's milk (in cooking but not as a drink); non-acidic bio yogurt; fromage frais, cottage cheese, mild tasting Cheddar, Edam, Gouda and mozzarella; free-range egg yolks, hard-boiled and mashed; a little tofu	Increase the range of dairy foods, but make sure cheeses are suitable for vegetarians. Avoid blue or unpasteurized cheeses. Offer well-cooked whole egg
NUTS AND SEEDS	–	–	–	If allergies are excluded, introduce finely ground nuts in casseroles or sauces. Spread smooth nut or seed butters on toast fingers
TEXTURE	Thin, completely smooth purées	Smooth, slightly thicker purées, not necessarily sieved	Thicker, smooth purées, moving on to finely mashed food	Coarsely mashed, moving on to finely chopped, and finger foods
MEALS PER DAY	1–2	2–3	3	3, plus 1 or 2 tiny healthy snacks
MILK	Breast feeds, or a minimum of 600 ml (1 pint) formula or special formula fortified soya baby milk	Breast feeds, or a minimum of 600 ml (1 pint) formula baby milk	Breast feeds, or a minimum of 500–600 ml (17 fl oz–1 pint) formula or follow-on milk	Breast milk at night and/or morning feeds, or a minimum of 500–600 ml (17 fl oz–1 pint) formula or follow-on milk

GETTING THE TEXTURE RIGHT

It is vital to get the consistency of your baby's food right. If it is too thick or coarse in the early stages, your baby will not be able to swallow his food. If it's too sloppy for too long, your baby will become a lazy eater who will be reluctant to eat food that requires much chewing. Be guided by your baby, but as he or she grows and progresses, aim to introduce more exciting textures – in the same way as you are broadening his or her experience of different tastes.

4 months 'Easy does it'

Begin with a sloppy, ultra smooth purée of baby rice or potato. Move on to purées of butternut squash, parsnip or carrot; thin porridge (not wheat or oats); banana, cooked apple or pear. (Illustrated bottom left: butternut squash purée)

5–6 months 'More please'

Give your baby purées with a slightly thicker texture but make sure they are still smooth. Try out new tastes, such as red lentils, avocado and papaya. (Illustrated bottom right: avocado purée)

6–9 months 'Lots of new tastes'

At this stage you can give puréed or mashed mixtures. Progress to coarser textures when your baby is ready to accept them. (Illustrated top left: mixed vegetable mash)

9–12 months 'I can feed myself'

At this stage, you can give your baby a wide variety of coarsely mashed or chopped meals, plus finger foods (see page 13) to pick up and eat. (Illustrated top right: Lentil Hotpot, page 46)

BATCH COOKING

As a baby eats tiny amounts, especially in the early days of weaning, it can be a great time-saver to make larger quantities of purée and freeze individual portions. These are ideal to take on outings, or to a baby minder or nursery if you return to work.

Make simple purées in quantity, or double up baby recipes then purée or mash. Take out a portion, cool and refrigerate for baby's next meal.

Spoon the rest into mini plastic containers, sections of ice cube trays, or small plastic bags. Cool, loosely covered, then seal well and label clearly with the date and type of food. Freeze and use within 6 weeks.

If using ice cube trays, open freeze until solid, then pop the cubes into a plastic bag, seal and label. Make up several different batches and as your baby's tastes broaden and appetite increases, mix different purée cubes together for greater variety.

Defrost mini dinners overnight in the refrigerator, then heat thoroughly and cool to the required temperature. Or microwave for a speedier option, but make sure that the food is heated through and stirred well to dispel any hot spots. Let cool for a few minutes and always check the temperature before serving.

READY-MADE BABY FOODS

These can be convenient, especially if you are out for the day or need to supply a meal for your child at day nursery. For most of your baby's meals, however, homemade foods are the best option – not least because they enable him to get used to the flavours of family meals. Bought baby foods also tend to work out much more expensive.

Keep a few cans and jars in reserve for emergencies, but keep an eye on the use-by date. Buy gluten-free and dairy-free foods for babies under 6 months. Choose foods without added sugar or sweetener. Check labels – drinks, in particular, often have a surprising amount of sugar or sweetener added.

BABY FOOD SAFETY

• Always wash hands thoroughly before preparing milk feeds and baby food.

• Wash chopping boards and utensils well – in a dishwasher if possible. Rinse hand-washed items, and change tea towels and dish cloths frequently. Ensure bottles and teats are clean before putting them into a sterilizer.

• Sterilize bottles and teats for milk feeds up until the age of 6 months. Use a steam sterilizer or microwave sterilizer, soak in sterilizing solution or boil in a pan of water for 3 minutes, making sure that all bottles, teats and caps are completely immersed in the water.

• Warm filled bottles by standing them in a jug of just boiled water. Only reheat bottles once.

• Refrigerate made up bottles of formula milk and use within 24 hours. If going out, keep them cool in an insulated bottle bag and use within 4 hours. Once baby starts to take milk from a bottle, use it within 1 hour.

• Reheat foods once only. Make sure it is piping hot all the way through. Stir well and leave until cool enough to give your baby.

• Always check the temperature of your baby's food before serving. The easiest way to do this is to put the spoon to your lip.

• When making your own baby foods, keep food loosely covered as it cools and refrigerate as soon as possible.

• If using a microwave, stir foods well to disperse hot spots.

ORGANIC FOODS FOR BABIES?

Potentially, babies have a greater exposure to chemical residues than most adults. This is because, weight for weight, babies consume far more fruit and vegetables, fruit juices, milk, eggs and other foods that are subject to the pesticides and antibiotics used in intensive farming. In addition, a child is more liable to absorb residues because their gastro-intestinal tract is more easily penetrated.

Fruit and vegetable crops are sprayed with pesticides to prevent plant diseases and increase a farmer's yield. Similarly, cows and chickens are given foodstuffs fortified with antibiotics, traces of which pass through to the milk and eggs. A growing consumer awareness of possible health risks associated with the use of these unnatural substances has led to the demand for organic foods. These are produced without the use of pesticides, growth hormones and additives, so you may prefer to buy them for your baby.

Due to demand, supermarkets are now stocking an increasing number of organic products. In addition to wider organic ranges of fresh vegetables and fruit, look for organic milk, cheese, eggs and canned foods too. Although organic foods are more expensive, the price differential is reducing as demand increases. If you have a local organic farm shop so much the better, as the food should be fresher and cheaper.

FOOD ALLERGIES

Some children are more susceptible than others to an allergic reaction triggered by a particular food. Those most at risk are from families with a history of an allergy, such as peanut allergy, other food allergy, asthma, eczema and/or hay fever. An estimated 1 in 10 children is prone to allergy.

The Department of Health recommends that infants who don't show signs of an allergic reaction but have a strong family history of allergy should be breastfed for at least 4–6 months and longer if possible. Weaning should be delayed until 5–6 months and then new foods introduced one at a time. Seek an expert diagnosis from your doctor or other professional health advisor before modifying a child's diet.

FOODS MOST LIKELY TO CAUSE ALLERGIES

• **Peanuts and other nuts** Peanuts can cause a particularly severe, potentially fatal, allergic reaction. Those who are prone must take great care to avoid peanuts, peanut butter, groundnut oil and unrefined peanut oil, particularly in ready-made meals and snacks. Food labels must be read carefully before purchase. Do not include peanuts in a baby's diet if there is a family history of hay fever, asthma or eczema, and only introduce carefully and under close supervision when your child is over 3 years. Seek advice from your local doctor about the introduction of other nuts in your child's diet.

• **Dairy products** Some children lack lactase – the enzyme that is needed to digest milk sugar. Tummy aches and diarrhoea are possible indications. Affected children may need to limit or omit cow's milk, cheese and butter from their diet. Soya milk and other soya products are suitable substitutes. Yogurt may be tolerated as the bacteria present produce their own lactase.

• **Gluten** Found in wheat, barley, rye and often oats, plus wheat-based products such as bread and pasta, this substance can cause problems. Babies with gluten intolerance may suffer from diarrhoea and tummy problems, leading on to damage to the lining of the intestine. If diagnosed, substitute rice cakes for bread, rice or corn noodles for wheat pasta, and buy rice or corn (maize) cereals for breakfast. Also use buckwheat, millet and sorghum.

• **Eggs** These can cause problems with a small number of children. Rashes, swelling and tummy upsets are possible indicators.

• **Citrus fruits and strawberries** A reaction to these may bring your baby out in a rash.

• **Additives** Hyperactivity in children is often attributed to certain artificial colourings, flavourings and sweeteners. The colouring agent, tartrazine, is one offender. Read food labels carefully before buying.

BUILDING A HEALTHY DIET

At first all your baby requires to stay healthy is milk – either breast milk or formula – but from around 4–6 months it will be necessary to introduce 'solid' foods to supplement the milk and meet your baby's changing nutritional needs. This is a time for great discovery but you will need to give your baby time to adjust, especially in those first few weeks of weaning. Some babies relish this new stage, while others prefer to wait. Some like the same food over and over again, whereas others are happy to try new tastes and quickly move on to thicker and coarser purées. By the time your baby reaches his first birthday your feeding routine should be well established, your baby may even have begun to feed himself and you will be able to share more and more family meals together.

CHOOSING THE RIGHT FOODS

Although appetites differ, we all need to eat a varied range of different foods. Unlike adults, children require the concentrated energy that fat provides and it is therefore not advisable to give children low-fat alternatives. A diet that is high in fibre isn't suitable for small children either, because too much fibre can fill up a tiny tummy before nutritional needs are met.

The key to a healthy diet is to make it as interesting and varied as possible and to encourage children to eat a wide range of foods. The healthy food pyramid (below, left) can help you towards a balanced diet. There are 4 important food groups: grains, cereals and bread; fruit and vegetables; protein-rich foods; fats and sugar. The food pyramid provides a guide to the proportion of these food groups to aim for. In essence, you need to include a much higher proportion of the foods in the lowest level than those towards the top. Only small amounts of the top layer are needed.

GRAINS, CEREALS AND BREAD

These are needed for energy. Choose from bread, breakfast cereals, maize, millet, couscous, potatoes, parsnips, yams, plantains, pasta and rice. Most children will happily tuck into these but make sure they leave room for other foods rich in protein, vitamins and minerals.

Under-ones can be introduced to gluten-free grains, such as rice and millet, once weaning is established. Progress from a tiny meal in those early days, to 2 and later 3 meals a day. From 6 months wheat products – such as pasta, flour and bread – may be introduced gradually. Purée, mash or chop food to begin with, adjusting the texture as your baby develops.

1–3 year olds may have progressed to 3, or even 4 mini portions a day depending on their appetite.

3–5 year olds may now be ready for 6 small helpings from this food group. Again, be guided by your child – a toddler's appetite can be quite erratic. Try to include a portion from this section with every meal, and one additional snack if your child gets hungry. Starchy vegetables, such as potatoes, parsnip and yams, may also be included in this group provided plenty of other fruit and vegetables have been eaten over the course of the day. For example, you could offer:

Breakfast: A bowl of cereal and slice of toast
Lunch: Oodles of Noodles (see page 75)
Snack: Date Muffin (see page 117) or a small hot cross bun
Tea: Kids' Kedgeree (see page 74)
Pudding: Mini Banana Castles (see page 102).

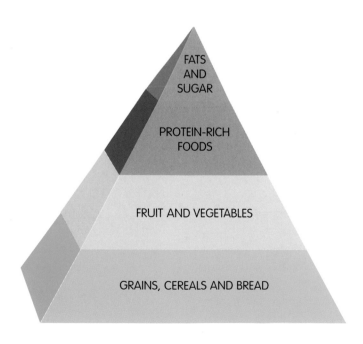

FATS AND SUGAR

PROTEIN-RICH FOODS

FRUIT AND VEGETABLES

GRAINS, CEREALS AND BREAD

HEALTHY FOOD PYRAMID

FRUIT AND VEGETABLES

These add colour and interest to our diet and are essential for providing a wide range of vitamins, minerals and fibre. Aim to work up to 5 small portions a day by the time your child is 2 years old. With some children this is no problem, with others it can seem like an impossible task. Some children will only eat fruit, others only vegetables, some any vegetable as long as it's not green! Be positive. Offer your children a variety of fruit and vegetables, make sure there is always the opportunity to eat more, but serve larger portions of any vegetable that you know is popular.

Offer starchy vegetables such as potatoes, yams, sweet potatoes; yellow-orange vegetables such as carrots, swede, sweetcorn, pumpkin, red and orange peppers; and green vegetables such as spinach, watercress, broccoli and peas.

Offer raw fruits as snacks rather than reach for the biscuit tin. Mix puréed, sliced or chopped fruits with yogurt for a speedy pudding. Keep a supply of puréed fruits in the freezer for quick ice cream sauces.

Choose from orchard fruits such as apples, pears, apricots and plums; soft berry fruits such as strawberries and raspberries; citrus fruits such as oranges, easy-peel satsumas and tangerines, and sweeter ruby grapefruit. Or try grapes, kiwi fruit, mangoes, peaches and melons.

Some children may be allergic to strawberries and oranges, so don't introduce these until your child is at least 6 months and then only in small amounts. Mix naturally sweet fruits with slightly sharper ones so that you don't need to add sugar.

Under-ones should be offered a selection of tastes and textures, working gradually towards 3 or 4 mini portions a day.

1–3 year olds may eat slightly larger portions. Gradually work up to 4 portions a day.

3–5 year olds have varying appetites. Aim for 5 portions a day, adjusting the portion size to suit your child. To put into practice:

Breakfast: Bowl of cereal with ½ banana, sliced, and a few sultanas

Lunch: Lentil Thatch with raw vegetable decoration (see page 60)

Pudding: Fruit yogurt with extra sliced or mashed strawberries

Snack: Few carrot and cucumber sticks with hummus

Tea: Marinated Tofu & Stir-fried Vegetables (see page 130).

PROTEIN-RICH FOODS

Children grow at such a rate, that they need more protein in relation to their body weight than adults. Protein is made up of 20 amino acids, eight of which cannot be manufactured from other proteins in the body. These are the 'essential amino acids' and are vital for growth and development. They are found in the following vegetarian foods:

• **Dairy and soya products** like milk, vegetarian cheese, yogurt, soya milk and yogurts, tofu and tempee.

• **Nuts** such as almonds, cashew nuts, hazelnuts, Brazil nuts, chestnuts, walnuts, pine nuts and peanuts, providing there is no family history of peanut or other allergies. Don't give whole or roughly chopped nuts to children under 5 years. From 9 months, grind nuts to a powder and add to purées, or mix with oil for a smooth nut paste. (See also page 33.)

• **Seeds** especially sunflower, sesame, pumpkin and linseed, and sprouted seeds such as alfalfa, chickpea and mung bean. Do not give whole seeds to children under 3 years for fear of choking. Instead grind to a smooth paste or butter with a little oil and offer in small quantities from 6–9 months.

- **Pulses** Peas, beans and lentils, including cooked dried pulses and canned ones. Buy canned pulses without added salt and sugar.
- **Eggs** Choose organic, free-range eggs.

Aim to work up to 4–6 servings per day once your child is 3 years old. This may seem a lot but, as children need and like to drink milk, the portions soon add up especially when they are eating 3 main meals. A 200 ml (⅓ pint) of milk is nutritionally equivalent to a 150 g (5 oz) pot of yogurt, or a 40 g (1½ oz) piece of cheese.

Under-ones will get the bulk of their protein from milk with smaller amounts from the gradual introduction of mini portions of lentils, mild-tasting cheeses, tofu, nuts (if appropriate) and seed butters.

1–3 year olds generally cut down on milk as a drink once breastfeeding stops or a feeder beaker takes the place of a bottle. Maintain milk as a drink and use milk and cheese in cooking. Serve yogurts and fromage frais as quick puddings or healthy snacks. Aim to include 2 helpings of milk or other dairy foods, plus 2 helpings of protein from the other groups.

3–5 year olds may want 2–3 servings of milk or milk products, plus 2–3 helpings of protein from the other groups. For example, you could offer:

On waking: 300 ml (½ pint) full-fat milk

Breakfast: Bowl of cereal with 100 ml (3½ fl oz) full-fat milk

Lunch: Cowboy Beans (see page 57), or baked beans on toast

Pudding: 100 g (3½ oz) fruity fromage frais

Tea: Marinated Tofu & Stir-fried Vegetables (see page 130)

Before bed: 150 ml (¼ pint) warm milk.

FATS AND SUGAR

Use foods rich in saturated fat – such as cream, butter, margarine and mayonnaise – sparingly. The same applies to sweet and sugary foods, such as cakes, biscuits, jams, honey, ice cream and sweet drinks. Some fat and sugar is useful to small children because of the concentrated energy that it provides but, rather than opt for sweet biscuits and cakes, choose foods that are naturally sweet such as ripe apples, pears or bananas. Try to avoid sweetening food for under-ones or they will crave sweet foods as they get older. Sugar also promotes tooth decay and in excess it leads to overweight in older children. Review the way you eat as a family and try to cut out sugar you add to tea or coffee, fruit salad or breakfast cereals. Aim to offer

sweet foods only after a meal and then brush your child's teeth or offer tiny cubes of cheese to neutralize the sugar. Try to avoid giving sweets as a reward.

Restrict fatty foods, such as crisps and similar snacks, that offer little other than fat. Instead, give them milk, cheese, nuts and seeds that contain fat but are rich in other nutrients too. Peanut butter on wholewheat toast will boost your child's energy levels for much longer than a 20–30 minute sugar burst supplied by a chocolate biscuit. If your child loves chips, make them oven chips rather than deep-fried ones. Add bread sticks, rice cakes, a homemade muffin, dried fruit or a few sprouting seeds to a packed lunchbox instead of crisps. Or give a child just a few crisps instead of the whole pack – with some vegetable sticks.

HOW BIG IS A PORTION?

When you first introduce solids to your baby, portion sizes will be minute tasters – about 1–2 teaspoons. As your baby progresses, so the amounts and frequency of meals gradually increases.

By the time your baby is 6–9 months he or she will probably be eating 3–4 tablespoons of solids or more, 2–3 times a day, with plenty of milk feeds still. Foods will consist largely of fruit, vegetables and grains.

By 9–12 months your baby will probably be eating 3–6 tablespoons of a savoury baby dinner followed by fruit, or fruit and yogurt, or fromage frais. Every baby will develop at his own pace and these amounts are merely a guide. If your baby eats more or less than this but is happy and growing well then continue offering those amounts. Your baby will soon show you when he's had enough.

Once your baby is 1 year old, you can begin to follow the healthy eating pyramid, offering foods in the proportions outlined. Quantifying portion sizes can be rather off-putting, especially if

your child has a small appetite. If your child is well and growing, the portion sizes he chooses to eat are right for him. One toddler may be satisfied with a quarter of an apple while a hungrier child may eat half, possibly even a whole apple. Similarly one child may want just a few toast fingers while another could eat a whole slice. If a child is not hungry no amount of coaxing will encourage him to eat more!

A good balanced diet should supply all the vitamins and minerals your child needs. For those with a poor appetite or going through a very fussy stage you may feel reassured to supplement your child's diet with specially formulated vitamin pills. Some health authorities recommend vitamin drops for babies over 6 months and these are available on prescription. Ask your health visitor or doctor for advice.

A DAY'S MENU FOR A 1–3 YEAR OLD

Breakfast: 1 scrambled egg, on 1 slice buttered wholemeal toast, plus a small glass diluted unsweetened orange juice
Morning snack: ½–1 rice cake
Lunch: Beat-the-clock Pizza (see page 85), with veggie sticks
Pudding: Fruit yogurt
Mid-afternoon snack: Plain hot cross bun with a beaker of milk
Tea: Vegetable Quartet with Parsnip Mash (see page 137)
Pudding: Dreamy Dunkers (see page 97)

Before bed: Small beaker of milk
Total servings: Protein 4; Fruit and vegetables 5; Grains/carbohydrate 4.

BUILDING FOR A HEALTHY FUTURE

Once your child approaches five and heads for school, things will never be the same. Their diet will now gradually work towards that of an adult with proportionately less fat and gradually more fibre, but they still need to eat foods that are nutrient dense, with plenty of energy, to cope with an active school day. Your child may also encounter peer pressure to eat the same foods as everyone else. While young children can happily say no to meat, many find it harder to refuse lots of sweets, biscuits and other junk food. The same works in reverse – some children decide that they don't want to eat meat, even though the rest of their family does.

A vegetarian diet is often healthier than one based on meat, especially if the latter is largely restricted to chicken nuggets and chips with few if any vegetables, followed by ice cream or puddings that exclude fruit. Many habits that are learnt in these early years may be continued through the teenage stage and into adult life. Research has shown that children brought up on a vegetarian diet grow just as well as those who eat meat. Furthermore, vegetarians may be less prone to heart disease, high blood pressure, obesity, diet-related diabetes, gallstones and certain forms of cancer in later life.

Ten healthy diet tips for young children
- Enjoy your food.
- Eat a varied range of foods from all the four main food groups.
- Eat plenty to grow and be physically active. (Be guided by your child's appetite and seek advice if worried.)
- Eat regularly and don't skip meals.
- Avoid adding sugar and salt to food. Keep sugary foods to mealtimes.
- Top up nutritional needs with healthy snacks.
- Include full-fat milk, cheese and other dairy products. (Young children shouldn't be on a low-fat diet.)
- Don't overdo the fibre – include white and brown bread, white and brown rice. (Don't add bran to a child's food.)
- Drink plenty of water throughout the day, as well as milk and unsweetened fruit juices.
- Brush young teeth regularly.

NUTRITIONAL KNOW HOW

A basic understanding of nutrients and their role in metabolism helps us to understand the importance of a balanced diet.

PROTEINS

Proteins are made up of amino acids, of which eight are essential and an extra ninth one, histidine, is vital for children. These essential amino acids can only be obtained from the foods we eat, unlike the others, which can be converted from amino acids stored by the body.

Every cell needs protein. It is required for the growth and repair of everything – from muscles and bones to hair and fingernails. Protein also helps to produce enzymes that aid digestion, antibodies that fight off infection, and hormones to keep the body working smoothly. If the intake of fats or carbohydrate is too low, then the body will draw on its protein and convert it into energy.

Only 'complete protein' from animal sources or soya products – such as cheese, eggs, soya beans and tofu – supplies all 8 essential amino acids. Other protein sources such as nuts, seeds and sprouting seeds, pulses and grains (with the exception of quinoa) are lacking in one or more of the essential amino acids. By eating a varied vegetarian diet, however, the mix of proteins will automatically provide all of the essential amino acids. It is not necessary to rely on complete protein foods, provided a range of proteins is consumed over the course of a day.

Protein boosters
- Serve baked beans on toast.
- Serve lentil dhal with rice .
- Add low sodium/salt yeast extract or dried yeast flakes to soups etc.
- Stir ground nuts or seeds, or nut/ seed butters into casseroles, pie fillings, burgers etc.
- Sprinkle soups with grated cheese.
- Add chopped hard-boiled egg to bean, lentil or vegetable salads.
- Add a little wheatgerm to pasta sauces (see left) and casseroles.

CARBOHYDRATES

These are the body's main source of fuel and energy and can be divided into three groups: sugars, starches and fibre.

SUGARS

These are found naturally in fruits (fructose) and milk (lactose), but it is refined sugar (sucrose) that we are more familiar with. Although sugar can be a great energy booster, its benefits are short lived. Sugar is rapidly absorbed by the blood stream to give your child a quick boost of energy, but this is followed by a slump as that energy is burnt up. Fluctuating blood sugar levels may cause a child to experience mood swings, temper tantrums and irritability. To minimize this effect, choose foods that provide other nutrients as well as sugar, such as ripe fruit, milk or vegetables. The energy from these foods will be released more slowly, so giving a more prolonged energy boost.

It is important to avoid adding sugar to under-ones' food. It is also wise to use it sparingly in toddlers' meals and later life, but there is no need to ban sugar altogether. A little sugar added to home baking, or to sweeten very sharp fruits during cooking is acceptable.

The real 'baddies' are bought cakes, biscuits, sweets, fizzy drinks and squashes that are loaded with sugar and provide 'empty calories' with little, if any other nutritional benefits. It is these foods that can cause serious tooth decay, Try to serve homemade cakes and biscuits as part of a special tea rather than as an everyday treat. Don't add sugar to drinks, and choose unsweetened fruit juices in preference to artificially sweetened squashes and cordials.

STARCHES

Sometimes known as complex carbohydrates, starches are broken down by the body into sugars during metabolism and used for energy. They take longer for the body to digest and absorb than simple sugars, so leaving your child feeling full and with more sustained energy.

Starches are present in grains such as wheat, oats, barley, rye, rice, maize (corn), buckwheat and millet; beans, peas and lentils; root vegetables such as carrots, parsnips, potatoes, beetroot, swede, turnips, yams and sweet potatoes; bananas and plantains.

FIBRE

Fibre is essential in the diet, although the amount needed is significantly less for young children. While fibre is important in a child's diet to maintain the health of the digestive tract and to prevent constipation, it is important not to overload tiny tummies. Fibrous foods can be bulky and filling, leaving little room for foods containing other essential nutrients. Too much fibre can also interfere with the absorption of some minerals such as zinc, iron and calcium.

Give children foods that contain soluble fibre such apples, pears, dried fruits, carrots, sweet potato, pulses, oats, brown rice and wholemeal bread. Offer a variety of these in small amounts. Not all grain products need be wholemeal. Many children find pastry made with a mix of white and wholemeal flour more palatable than wholemeal pastry, and are happy to eat sandwiches made with one slice of white and one slice of brown bread. Choose easy-cook brown rice and, if your child doesn't like wholemeal pasta, stick to the familiar refined variety.

Don't include insoluble fibre found in All bran cereals and wheat bran as it is too difficult and too abrasive for a child to digest.

Recipes that provide a good mix of fibre and other nutrients include: Cowboy Beans (see page 57); Lentil Thatch (see page 60); Chestnut Sofrito (see page 136); Pink Blush Jellies (see page 98); Rainbow Sundaes (see page 100).

FATS AND OILS

These are a valuable source of concentrated energy for children, containing more than twice the amount of calories as the same weight of carbohydrates or proteins. Fats are also needed to maintain cells, produce hormones, and to provide the fat-soluble vitamins A, D, E and K. The best sources are foods that contain other nutrients as well – such as milk, cheese, eggs, nuts and oils. Too many foods laden with 'hidden' fats and sugars – such as cakes, biscuits and pastries – can lead to obesity and heart disease. Fats are made up of saturated fatty acids, polyunsaturated fats and mono-unsaturated fats.

SATURATED FATTY ACIDS

These are found in milk, cheese and eggs. Buy full-fat milk and cheese in preference to low-fat versions for children under 2, to ensure they are getting enough of the fat-soluble vitamins. Semi-skimmed products can be introduced slowly from 2 years if your child has a varied diet and is growing well, but it is better to continue with full-fat dairy products until they are 5 years old, unless there is a weight problem.

POLYUNSATURATED FATS

These can be divided into:

Essential omega-3 fat derived from linolenic acid and essential for the brain and retina of the eye during early development. Breast milk is rich in this fat, but it is often lacking in a child's diet. Essential omega-3 fat is found in green leafy vegetables, including broccoli and beans; wholegrains; sweet potato; walnuts, pumpkin seeds, olives and their oils; rapeseed oil.

Omega-6 fat derived from linoleic acid and needed for cell structure and blood flow. Found in soya, corn, olive and rapeseed oils, avocados and beans.

MONO-UNSATURATED FATS

Help to keep arteries healthy and are found mainly in olives and olive oil, avocados, most nuts and their oils, sesame seeds and their oil.

VITAMINS

Vitamins are vital for good health and essential for the correct development and function of the brain and nervous system. With the exception of vitamin D, they cannot be manufactured by the body so they must be supplied by the foods we eat.

VITAMIN A

Needed to: aid normal cell division; for growth and protein manufacture; to maintain mucous membranes of the respiratory, digestive and urinary tract; for good eyesight and immunity. This vitamin is also an important antioxidant that helps protect cells from free radical damage.

Found in: eggs, cheese and milk. In fruit and vegetables it is present in the form of beta-carotene, a carotenoid pigment which is converted by the body into vitamin A. As a guide, the

more vibrant the vegetable the more beta-carotene it contains. Carrots, red peppers, mangoes, some types of melon, peaches, apricots, spinach and kale are good sources. Vitamin A is also added to margarines.

Watchpoint: Weight for weight, six times more beta-carotene is needed to produce the same amount of vitamin A (retinol) as that from eggs, milk and cheese.

B VITAMINS

This group includes thiamin (B1), riboflavin (B2), niacin (B3), pantothenic acid, pyridoxine (B6), biotin, cyanocobalamin (B12) and folate (folic acid).

Needed to: aid growth, metabolism and energy production and to keep each cell healthy. All of the B group, except B12 and folate, are involved in the release of energy from food. Vitamin B12 is needed for red blood cell formation; calcium, magnesium and selenium metabolism; zinc absorption and nerve function. Folate keeps arteries healthy and is vital for the production of haemoglobin, the pigment in red blood cells. Folate or folic acid is also necessary before conception and during early pregnancy to help prevent neural defects.

Found in: All B vitamins, except B12, occur in yeast; wholegrain cereals, especially wheat germ; nuts; beans, peas and lentils;

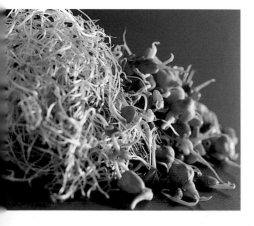

seeds and sprouted seeds; green vegetables; also avocados, mushrooms, bananas, eggs and dairy products. Vitamin B12 is available from dairy foods, eggs, fortified breakfast cereals, low-salt yeast extracts and soya milks.

Watchpoint: All B vitamins are water soluble so don't throw cooking liquids away but use in sauces and gravies. Vitamin B12 is the only B vitamin that can be stored by the body.

VITAMIN C

Needed to: make the protein collagen – essential for healthy skin, bones and cartilage. Vitamin C aids the absorption of iron, too. It can also help to produce the two neurotransmitters: noradrenaline which aids blood flow; and serotonin which aids sleep and alleviates stress – helpful with young children! This vitamin is also an important antioxidant that helps protect cells from damage.

Found in: citrus fruit, such as oranges and orange juice; strawberries, red and blackcurrants; kiwi fruit, pineapple and melon; peppers, tomatoes, cauliflower, broccoli and Brussels sprouts; small amount in potatoes.

Watchpoint: Vitamin C is easily destroyed by oxidation so prepare vegetables just before cooking. It is water soluble too, so steaming is the best cooking method. Keep cooking times to the minimum as vitamin C is also heat sensitive; serve fruit and vegetables raw if possible.

VITAMIN D

Needed to: aid the body's absorption of minerals, particularly calcium, iron, phosphorous and magnesium.

Found in: milk, dairy products and eggs; cold-pressed vegetable oils; nuts; fortified breakfast cereals, soya milks and margarine.

Watchpoint: The effect of sunlight on the skin enables our bodies to produce vitamin D. As little as 30 minutes' play outside can be sufficient to meet your child's daily vitamin D requirement. Take extra care of young skins in the summer and protect with a sunscreen.

VITAMIN E

Needed as: an antioxidant to protect and prolong the life of cells. It can also aid fertility and immunity, and helps keep red blood cells healthy.

Found in: eggs; soya beans; wholegrain cereals and wheat germ; nuts and seeds; vegetable oils and avocados. Vitamin E deficiency is rare but may occur in premature babies.

Watchpoint: A little nut butter spread on toast, or a little oil in lentil mixtures or hummus, easily makes up a child's daily requirement.

VITAMIN K

Needed to: form certain proteins and for healthy blood clotting; also required for strong bones.

Found in: egg yolk; green leafy vegetables, broccoli, cauliflower, turnips and tomatoes; beans sprouts and beans; wholegrains; rapeseed and olive oil. It is also produced in the intestine by bacterial synthesis.

Watchpoint: This vitamin is given as an injection to newborn babies.

MINERALS

We need minerals to aid the work vitamins do, to maintain a healthy immune system, and strengthen bones and teeth. Minerals also help control the composition of body fluids and cells. Our bodies can draw on stores laid down in muscles, the liver and bones over short periods – important if a child is going through a difficult eating stage.

CALCIUM

Needed for: healthy bones and teeth – all but 1% is utilized for this. A small amount combines with magnesium to promote the

well being of every cell. Calcium is also needed for healthy muscle and nerve function, blood clotting, and vitamin B12 absorption. If a child loses appetite then the body can draw on stores in the bones. Once normal eating resumes calcium will re-enter the bones.

Found in: milk, dairy products and eggs; dark green leafy vegetables; root vegetables; beans, peas and lentils; nuts and seeds; wholegrain foods, dried fruits and bread.

Watchpoint: Eat calcium-rich foods together with foods that contain vitamin D to aid the absorption of this important mineral. Too much fibre in the diet – and tannin which is present in tea – may inhibit the absorption of calcium.

IODINE

Found in: dairy products, eggs, fruit and vegetables (except the cabbage family), pineapple, raisins, wholegrain foods.

Needed for: production of the thyroid hormone.

IRON

Needed for: the production of haemoglobin, the oxygen-carrying red pigment in blood cells. Iron is also essential for the manufacture of certain enzymes, to boost immunity, for energy production and liver function. Iron is a very important mineral and an adequate intake is vital for good health. If your child's diet is deficient in iron, anaemia may result.

Found in: leafy green vegetables; wholemeal bread; molasses; egg yolk; dried fruit; tofu; lentils and pulses; fortified breakfast cereals and soya milk.

Watchpoint: To aid absorption, eat foods that contain iron with foods that are rich in vitamin C. Adding a portion of vitamin C-rich foods to a meal can increase the absorption of iron from plant sources six fold. Phytic acid, found in wheat bran and brown rice, can inhibit absorption. Iron deficiency anaemia is no more common among vegetarians than the rest of the population.

Iron boosters
- Serve a glass of orange juice with a meal.
- Offer fresh fruit or fruit salad for dessert. Citrus fruits, strawberries and kiwi fruit are excellent vitamin-C rich iron boosters.
- Add orange segments or a squeeze of lemon juice to lentils and pulses just before serving.
- Enrich slow-cooked bean or vegetable casseroles with fresh tomato sauce, or a tablespoon or two of molasses.
- Stir-fry tofu with broccoli.
- Serve easy-cook brown rice instead of wholegrain rice.
- Add a range of leafy green vegetables to salads and stir-fries.

MAGNESIUM

Needed for: bone construction, to aid enzymes in the release of energy, the manufacture of insulin and proteins, and the removal of waste products.
Found in: wholegrain cereals; dried figs, nuts and pulses; green leafy vegetables.

POTASSIUM

Needed to: regulate blood pressure and heart beat. Potassium is also essential for the transmission of nerve impulses, the production of protein, and works with sodium to maintain fluid and acidity balance in cells.
Found in: avocados, bananas, citrus fruits and dried fruits; nuts and seeds; pulses; whole grains, green leafy vegetables, tomatoes and potatoes.

SELENIUM

Needed as: an antioxidant to protect cells from damage. Vital for sexual development.
Found in: dairy products and egg yolk; green leafy vegetables, garlic and mushrooms; beans and peas; nuts and wholegrains.

ZINC

Needed for: many enzyme reactions, the immune system, as part of the make up of DNA and RNA, to aid growth, and the development of reproductive organs – particularly in children and adolescents.
Found in: green vegetables; sesame and pumpkin seeds; peanuts; lentils and wholegrain cereals; dairy produce and eggs.
Watchpoint: The phytic acid in wholegrain cereals can hinder the absorption of the zinc present, so this mineral is more readily absorbed from dairy produce and eggs. Consequently, children following a vegan or dairy-free diet may need to take zinc supplements to prevent a deficiency of this vital mineral. If applicable, consult your doctor first.

SALT

Most of us eat more salt than we need to. In later life a high intake can cause high blood pressure and increase the risk of strokes, heart disease and kidney failure. Children, particularly under-ones, are unable to cope with high concentrations of salt because their kidneys are not fully matured. For this reason it is vital not to add salt to a baby's food and to avoid using salty stock cubes or processed foods that are high in salt.

Try to prevent your child from developing a taste for salt. For toddlers, flavour foods with spices and herbs or a little garlic instead. Some foods such as polenta do require seasoning during cooking, but a little salt will suffice. Discourage children from adding salt at the table and review your inclination to do so – children are inclined to copy.

Processed foods – notably baked beans, canned soups, crisps, even breakfast cereals – probably contain much more salt than you imagine.

Read the label. The recommended daily amount of sodium for a toddler is 500 mg, which is equivalent to ¼ teaspoon salt or 1.75 g. To calculate the salt content from the sodium (mg weight) stated on your child's favourite bought products, multiply the sodium figure by 2.5 to give the weight of salt in grams (g).

WHAT'S IN A LABEL?

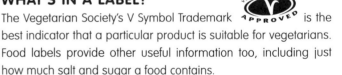

The Vegetarian Society's V Symbol Trademark is the best indicator that a particular product is suitable for vegetarians. Food labels provide other useful information too, including just how much salt and sugar a food contains.

Ingredients are given in descending order of weight, so the product contains more of the first ingredient on the list than subsequent ones. Be wary if sugar appears at the top: it may be in the form of sucrose, glucose, maltose, dextrose, glucose syrup, lactose, corn syrup, hydrolized starch, inverted sugar, fructose or concentrated fruit juice, or a combination of these. 1 teaspoon of sugar is equivalent to 5 ml or 4 g.

Salt is usually listed as sodium. It is a surprising ingredient in many products, including breakfast cereals. Many processed foods contain high levels of sodium and are inappropriate for small children (see Salt, above).

Be wary of certain forms of labelling. For example, in a 'strawberry flavoured yogurt', there may not be any actual strawberries, just added flavour. By law, these packs cannot show a picture of the main flavouring ingredient, so if you can't see a strawberry on the pot you are unlikely to find any inside!

Additives are usually listed as E numbers; the label may also state what kind of colouring, preservative, flavouring or emulsifier is contained. Avoid E120, E441 and E542 as these are never from vegetarian sources. Emulsifiers may not be vegetarian. (See also Additives, opposite page.)

Date marks, sell-by and use-by dates indicate how fresh a product is. Adhere to these, follow storage instructions and – if in doubt – throw the product out!

STANDBYS FOR A HEALTHY DIET

Keep a selection of the following foods and you will always be able to make a quick, healthy supper for the family in around the time it would take you to pop out and pick up a takeaway!

IN THE CUPBOARD:
• selection of grains to include easy-cook brown rice, bulgar wheat, oats, barley, millet grains or flakes, plain and self-raising white and wholemeal flours
• longlife packs of tofu
• red, green and Puy lentils
• dried or canned pulses without added salt and sugar, such as chick peas, red kidney beans, cannellini or borlotti beans
• pasta, couscous and polenta
• seeds such as sesame, sunflower and pumpkin, and tahini
• nuts such as ground almonds, whole hazelnuts and cashews;

peanut butter (unless allergy is a consideration)
• canned tomatoes, passata, tomato purée and low sugar/salt tomato ketchup
• oils such as sunflower, rapeseed and olive oils
• salt-free or low-salt stock cubes
• garlic
• spices such as ground cumin, coriander, paprika, cinnamon, nutmeg and allspice
• dried herbs such as rosemary, sage, bay leaves and marjoram (although better to grow your own and use fresh)
• white and brown sugars and molasses
• dried fruits such as sultanas, raisins, apricots and dates
• extras such as yeast flakes, low salt yeast extract, malt extract

IN THE VEGETABLE RACK:
• potatoes and onions
• carrots and other root vegetables

IN THE FRIDGE:
• full-fat milk; hard vegetarian cheeses such as Cheddar, and soft vegetarian cheeses such as mozzarella; fromage frais, plain or fruit yogurt
• free-range eggs
• butter or margarine
• leafy green vegetables such as broccoli and cabbage
• unsweetened fruit juice
• sugar-free fruit spreads; low-sugar jam

IN THE FREEZER:
• vegetables such as sweetcorn, spinach, peas, broad beans
• thick-cut oven chips (not ones coated with animal fat)
• selection of berry fruits or mixed bags of summer fruits
• dairy ice cream
• carton of full-fat milk, pack of butter or margarine, and a bag of ready-grated Cheddar cheese – for emergencies
• sliced wholemeal bread, rolls and pitta breads

IN THE FRUIT BOWL:
• Bananas, naturally sweet dessert apples, ripe pears
• Oranges, easy-peel satsumas or tangerines
• Melon, grapes, kiwi fruit

NON-VEGETARIAN FOODS TO AVOID

If you wish to adhere strictly to a vegetarian diet, don't be caught out by hidden sources of animal products.

ADDITIVES Check labels for added emulsifiers, stabilizers and colourings – indicated by listed E numbers. Not all are derived from vegetarian sources. Avoid E120, E441 and E542 which are from animal sources. E901 and E904 are suitable for vegetarians but not vegans. Be wary of E631 and E920 which may be derived from either animal or vegetarian sources. A more comprehensive list of additives that may be unsuitable for vegetarians may be obtained from the Vegetarian Society.

CHEESES Avoid those made with rennet, an animal derived enzyme from a calf's stomach lining which is used to separate milk into curds and whey. Look out for cheeses with the vegetarian symbol 👁 – which indicates that they have been produced using a vegetarian alternative to rennet. Most popular cheeses are now available in vegetarian form, although you may need to shop around as not all supermarkets stock them.

CHIPS Some oven-ready chips and those from takeaways may be coated or fried in animal fat.

CHOCOLATE This may include whey and non-vegetarian emulsifiers. Milk chocolate coatings may contain whey that is not listed on the label.

CRÈME FRAÎCHE Check product labels as low-fat or reduced-fat varieties sometimes have gelatine added to thicken them.

EGGS Choose free-range eggs – preferably organically produced. Avoid battery-farmed eggs. Be aware that products which contain eggs, such as mayonnaise and egg noodles, may have been manufactured using battery-farmed eggs. However, an increasing number are produced using free-range eggs to make them suitable for vegetarians, including some of the Quorn range of products.

FOOD COLOURINGS Many children's sweets contain E120 or cochineal – the red food colouring derived from crushed insects.

E124 Ponceau 4R is acceptable and sometimes known as Cochineal Red A. Also suitable is E162 – made with beetroot juice.

GELATINE This is made from animal ligaments, tendons and bones. Gelatine is found in most set desserts, packs of fruit flavoured jelly, some jellied sweets, some dual yogurt and fruit pots, some ice creams and confectionery, even bought guacamole (avocado dip). Choose products set with guar gum instead or, if making your own jellies or mousses, use agar agar or Vege-Gel. Also avoid aspic powder and Aka E441.

ICE CREAM Some types include animal fats. Look for 'Dairy' on the label and check that only milk fats have been used. Some ice creams contain battery farmed eggs and gelatine. Watch out for E numbers and whey too. If in doubt, only buy ice cream with the vegetarian symbol 👁.

JELLY This is usually made with gelatine. Make your own and set with Vege-Gel.

MARGARINE Not all margarines are made purely with vegetable products. Some rather astonishingly have fish oils, animal fats, even gelatine added. Read the labels carefully and buy only those with the vegetarian symbol 👁.

PESTO This popular basil sauce may be mixed with Parmesan made with animal rennet. Choose a brand made with vegetarian Parmesan, possibly carrying the vegetarian symbol 👁.
Alternatively, make your own using ground pine nuts, chopped fresh basil, grated vegetarian Parmesan and olive oil.

SUET Choose vegetable suet in place of animal suet. It has the added advantage that it's much lower in fat too.

WHEY A by-product of the cheese industry, this may be produced using animal rennet.

WORCESTERSHIRE SAUCE Most brands contain anchovies, but vegetarian versions are available in healthfood shops.

YOGURTS These may contain gelatine. Check the labels.

FEEDING YOUR TODDLER & PRE-SCHOOL CHILD

Once the foundations for a healthy diet are laid, your toddler should be enjoying a wide range of foods with a variety of tastes and textures.

Continue to broaden your child's diet and offer tasters of your own meals. Little children can often surprise you and tuck into things you wouldn't expect them to like at all. Encourage children to try new foods and learn not to say ' I don't like it' until they have tried it. Obviously, you should avoid giving them very hot and spicy foods. Like adults, toddlers' appetites vary. Be guided by your child and don't be alarmed if your child appears to eat very little some days – the hungry days and the not so hungry days usually balance out.

As children grow so rapidly, foods need to be nutrient dense for maximum energy, protein, vitamins and minerals. Encourage children to eat three healthy balanced meals a day and boost their energy and nutritional needs with healthy snacks. It's amazing how a mid-afternoon snack can help revitalize a tired and fractious toddler.

Make mealtimes enjoyable – a time to chat and eat – not something to rush through or do in front of the television. Try to eat together as a family as often as possible. If work commitments make this too difficult during the week, then feed the children together and make time to share meals with them over the weekend.

Mealtimes may be messy as your child learns how to use a spoon and fork. Shield the area beneath your baby's high chair or booster seat with a plastic mat or towel and offer foods that stay on a spoon well, plus easy to eat finger foods.

For 1–3 year olds, aim for:
• 3–4 helpings of grains and starchy cereals to include bread, rice, pasta, breakfast cereals and potatoes
• 3–4 helpings of fruit and vegetables
• 1–2 helpings of dairy and/or soya foods such as cheese, eggs, yogurt, and tofu
• Plenty of milk to drink. Aim for a minimum of 350 ml (12 fl oz) full-fat cow's milk or fortified soya milk. If your child won't drink milk, give them 2 extra servings of dairy or soya products (as above.)
• 1 helping of pulses, lentils, dried or canned beans, finely ground seeds or nuts (provided peanut or other allergy isn't a consideration)
As your toddler grows and develops, so their dietary needs change.

For children of 3 years and over, aim for:
• 4–6 servings of grains and cereals to include bread, rice, pasta, breakfast cereals and potatoes
• 3–5 helpings of fruit and vegetables, to include at least one green vegetable a day, and a little dried fruit. Try to include fruit and vegetables in each meal and offer fruit instead of biscuits as a healthy snack between meals. Include potatoes, beans or peas if not counted as starchy alternatives to grains.
• 3 helpings of dairy or soya foods such as full-fat milk or semi-skimmed cow's milk, cheese, eggs, yogurt, tofu, fortified soya milk
• 1–2 helpings of nuts, pulses and seeds, including homemade nut butters or ready-made tahini or smooth peanut butter, lentils and beans. Avoid nuts if allergy is a consideration.

3 DAY PLANNER FOR 1–3 YEAR OLDS

	DAY 1	DAY 2	DAY 3
ON WAKING	Beaker of full-fat milk	Beaker of full-fat milk	Beaker of full-fat milk
BREAKFAST	Scrambled egg on toast Beaker of orange juice diluted with water	Porridge topped with a spoonful of fruit spread Buttered toast fingers Beaker of orange juice diluted with water	Bowl of cereal with milk Kiwi fruit (eaten 'boiled egg' style) Beaker of water
MID-MORNING SNACK	Fruit Smoothie (see page 108)	Few squares of cheese and a mini box of raisins Beaker of full-fat milk	Rice cake, carrot and cucumber sticks Beaker of apple juice diluted with water, or plain water
LUNCH	Lentil Thatch (see page 60) Mini dessert apple, cored and filled with diced dried fruits, baked and served with custard, ice cream or fromage frais Beaker of water or milk	Takeaway Tortilla (see page 113), plus a soft bread roll Peeled satsuma or a few strawberries Beaker of water or milk	Small baked potato filled with Cowboy Beans (see page 57) or canned baked beans Fruit yogurt Beaker of water
MID-AFTERNOON SNACK	Few plain crisps, carrot and cucumber sticks Beaker of full-fat milk	Small bowl of cereal with milk Beaker of apple juice diluted with water, or plain water	Date Muffin, (see page 117) or mini hot cross bun Beaker of full-fat milk
TEA	Open (cheese) Sandwich (see page 95) Small fruit yogurt Beaker of apple juice diluted with water, or plain water	Cauliflower & Lentil Dhal with Tomatoes (see page 135) Scoop of fruit sorbet or a homemade lolly (see page 107) Beaker of water	Roast Pumpkin & Risotto (see page 129) Mini Banana Castles (see page 102) Beaker of water
BEFORE BED	Beaker of full-fat milk	Beaker of full-fat milk	Beaker of full-fat milk

3 DAY PLANNER FOR 3 YEAR OLDS AND OVER

	DAY 1	DAY 2	DAY 3
BREAKFAST	Smooth peanut butter or seed butter on toast Small fruit yogurt Beaker of orange juice	Bowl of cereal with milk Sliced apple Beaker of orange juice or water	Boiled egg and toast fingers Beaker of orange juice
MID-MORNING SNACK	Banana Beaker of water	2 plain digestive biscuits Beaker of full-fat milk	Fruit Smoothie (see page 108)
LUNCH	Mini Pasta Salad (see page 111) Pink Blush Jelly (see page 98) Banana and Chocolate Chip Muffin (see page 117) Beaker of water	Cowboy Beans (see page 57) Fruity fromage frais Beaker of water	Bean & Pesto Pots (see page 68) Fruity fromage frais Beaker of water
MID-AFTERNOON SNACK	Few bread sticks with a little hummus for dipping Beaker of semi-skimmed or full-fat milk	Few dried fruits and a rice cake Beaker of water	Few mixed dried fruits Beaker of water
TEA	Kid's Kedgeree (see page 74) Scoop of ice cream topped with a smooth fruit sauce (puréed strawberries or cooked dried apricots) Beaker of orange juice	Vegetable Quartet with Parsnip Mash (see page 137) Fruit salad (eg sliced kiwi fruit, orange segments and diced melon) Beaker of fruit juice or water	Oodles of Noodles (see page 75) or Cabbage Cups with Creamy Carrot Sauce (see page 81) Date & Orange Fool (see page 101) Beaker of fruit juice or water
BEFORE BED	Beaker of semi-skimmed or full-fat milk	Beaker of semi-skimmed or full-fat milk	Beaker of semi-skimmed or full-fat milk

COPING WITH A FUSSY EATER

As your toddler matures and develops so their tastes and preferences are liable to change, and your loveable baby may transform into a mealtime tyrant! It can be a very frustrating time. To witness the meal you have prepared, played with, spat out, or even thrown on the floor can be exasperating. Some children find comfort in a narrow repetitious diet and seem to thrive on surprisingly few foods. This may last for a few weeks, even a few months, before it ends – often quite suddenly. Perversely my own children seemed to lose their appetite when they were going through a growth spurt, a time when you would expect them to be ravenously hungry. Coping with a fussy eater can be stressful, especially if you have other demands such as a young baby who wakes at night.

- Try to work out why your child dislikes a particular food so much. Is it the taste or texture, or does the food really make your child feel ill. If it's the latter, speak to your health visitor or doctor.
- Talk to other parents – it can be a great comfort to know you're not alone!
- If your child won't eat proper meals, resist the temptation to give them snacks between meals. If they become hungry, offer a piece of fruit, slice of bread and butter, or some veggie sticks and cheese – not a chocolate biscuit or bag of crisps. Don't give in otherwise your child will quickly catch on and refuse all main meals knowing that you will later meet their demand for sweet 'empty calorie' alternatives.
- Make time to sit down and eat with your child. Switch on the answerphone or simply ignore the telephone that always seems to ring the minute you dish up. Have everything on the table so that you don't need to keep getting up and down.
- Try not to get cross. Children soon learn that refusing food will be met with a reaction of some kind – especially from a tired parent – and use it as a way of gaining attention.
- Never force a child to eat – this never works. It's amazing how many adults still refuse a particular food because they were made to eat it as a child.
- Offer a range of foods, and only a small portion of any food your child dislikes. At some stage he may surprise you!
- Praise your child for what he has eaten rather than focus on what remains. When he has clearly had enough, take away the plate, even if there's a lot left. No child will voluntarily starve himself.
- Offer just one drink with a meal so that your child doesn't fill up with liquids.
- Consider which meals your child responds best to. You may find that a toddler will eat a better breakfast when older children have gone to school and the house is quiet. Or perhaps your child is just too tired to eat tea, especially if it is delayed. In this case, providing an earlier meal may help.
- If you are particularly concerned, keep a record of what your child eats over the course of a week, rather than focus on one meal. There may be more than just mini fromage frais or biscuits to the diet after all! If it's worse than you thought, discuss the food record with your health visitor or doctor. They will check your child's weight and height gain. Reassuringly, most paediatricians agree that children will not starve if there is food about!

ENCOURAGING A CHILD TO EAT MORE VEGETABLES

- Offer raw vegetables instead of cooked ones, or try reducing the cooking time slightly so that they are still a little crunchy. The novelty of eating corn-on-the-cob may be just enough to encourage a child to try something new.

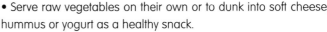

- Serve up tiny portions of a range of vegetables or invite your child to help himself from a plate of mixed vegetables. Some children prefer food to be kept separate rather than mixed together, as in a stir-fry.
- Purée mixed vegetables to disguise them. Serve with pasta, or make smooth vegetable soups and serve with fun-shaped croûtons or bread.
- Serve raw vegetables on their own or to dunk into soft cheese, hummus or yogurt as a healthy snack.
- Add vegetables to slow-cooked casseroles so that they take on the flavours of other ingredients, such as herbs and mild spices.

ENCOURAGING A CHILD TO EAT MORE FRUIT

- Keep an inviting fruit bowl – making sure it is easily visible and at a height your child can reach.
- Offer a piece of fruit at breakfast when your child is hungry.
- Take ready-prepared fruit in a small plastic box when you go out and leave the biscuits behind!
- Freeze fruit purées in sections of an ice cube tray and defrost a few at a time in the microwave for a quick ice cream sauce.

- Make up fruit lollies with puréed fruit or fruit juices.
- Stop buying biscuits and crisps so that your children get used to having fruit instead.
- Start a star chart – the family member who eats the most fruit over a week gets to choose Friday night's supper.

TIME FOR ACTION

If you feel that your family meals are becoming more like a war zone, it's time to take action. Involve the family and get everyone's support – mealtimes disrupted by a small child are frustrating for everyone. Talk to your fussy eater and explain that from next Monday things are going to be different:

• Work out the week's menu and hide the biscuits and crisps so that there can be no secret snacking. Try to include foods that your child will eat, and that the whole family enjoys too.

• Set yourself a time scale – perhaps 1 or 2 weeks – and if things have improved, plan a special outing or picnic.

• Explain to your child that if the meal is disrupted he will be told to leave the table and go to another room (but not one with a TV).

• If your child refuses to eat, don't make it an issue, but do make sure they realise there won't be anything else until the next meal.

• Don't get involved in bargaining. Never give in to 'I'll eat my tea if it's in front of the TV!'... or 'I'll sit at the table if I can have peanut butter sandwiches'.

• Offer small portions to your fussy eater so that the amount of food doesn't look overwhelming, and offer praise when it's due.

It's hard, but don't give in. If your child won't eat anything, stay calm, bring the next meal forward a little and try again. Be positive, things can only get better!

MAKING MEALTIMES FUN AGAIN

In many cases, definitive action isn't necessary. Often all that is needed to encourage a child to eat more is to do something a little different. Pack up a picnic and eat it at the park, or cover the kitchen or garden table with blankets or tablecloths and eat tea in your camp – under, rather than on the table!

Invite a favourite relative over and encourage your child to help set the table and make it look special. Or ask a friend with a good appetite over for lunch or tea and hopefully your child may learn by example or peer group pressure! Or involve your child in preparing tea for the rest of the family or a dollies' or teddy bears' tea party.

MAKE TIME FOR BREAKFAST

For young children who are off to day nursery or playgroup, breakfast can become a very hurried affair. Try to build in time for your child to eat this important first meal of the day – it may be 12 hours since they last ate! Recent research has shown that children who eat a good breakfast perform better at school, too.

Your child's blood sugar level will be low after a night's sleep, so offer naturally sweet fruits or fruit juices, or add dried fruits to breakfast cereals. Try to avoid sweet and refined breakfast cereals. Instead offer children healthier cereals such as Weetabix, baby muesli or porridge, ideally served without added sugar or just a light sprinkling over porridge. (A teaspoon of sugar will be much less than the 4 teaspoons in a portion of some honey-coated cereals!) Fortified breakfast cereals are a useful source of vitamin B12, particularly for children on a vegan diet, if they are served with soya milk.

Alternatively, offer bread or toast spread with a homemade nut or seed butter (providing allergy isn't a consideration), or a bought fruit spread. The vitamin and mineral content of brown and white bread is similar because the latter is fortified during processing, but wholemeal bread offers longer lasting energy.

Boost calcium levels by serving a drink of milk, mini fromage frais or yogurt. Provide very hungry children with a cooked breakfast, such as a well-cooked boiled or scrambled egg.

A child who eats a well balanced breakfast should be ready for the action-packed day ahead and hopefully will not crave something sweet mid morning – a sure sign that blood sugar levels are low.

BREAKFAST BOOSTERS

Many children eat the same breakfast every day, but there are many alternatives you can offer to provide variety. Try the following:

• Eggy Bread Dominoes (see page 86)

• Fruit Smoothies (see page 108)

• Rainbow Sundaes (see page 100) and Date & Orange Fools (see page 101). These can both be made the day before and refrigerated overnight. The date mixture from the fool is delicious spread on toast, too.

• As a change from oat porridge, try millet flakes mixed with full-fat milk (in the same proportions as oat porridge). Simmer, stirring continuously for 4–5 minutes. Serve sweetened with low-sugar jam, date purée, mashed bananas, fruit spread or a little sugar.

• Defrost a cube or two of baby fruit purée (see page 15) in the microwave, and mix with some fromage frais or Greek yogurt. Or spoon the fruit purée on to millet or oat porridge, or baby rice.

• Make your own seed spread for topping toast. Brush a nonstick frying pan with olive oil, add 3 tablespoons of mixed sesame and sunflower seeds and cook, stirring frequently, for 2–3 minutes until lightly browned. Then grind with 2 tablespoons of mixed sultanas and raisins and enough olive oil to make a smooth paste. Store in a jar in the fridge up to 1 week. Nut spreads can be made in the same way too.

• If you have a juicer, use it to make fresh juices for breakfast. Good combinations are carrot and apple; orange and banana; orange and melon. Use one of each (or a wedge in the case of melon) and top up all juices with a little water.

I'M THIRSTY MUM...

Aim to offer a range of drinks and include full-fat milk, water and unsweetened fruit juices, diluting these with water for children under the age of 2 years. As fruit juices can be quite high in natural sugars and fruit acids, it is better to offer these only at mealtimes and then to brush your child's teeth afterwards.

Milk is still a very important drink. Try to include at least 350 ml (12 fl oz) of milk a day in your child's diet. Or better still: 600 ml (1 pint) which will provide your child with enough riboflavin and calcium, half their daily protein requirement and valuable amounts of vitamin A, thiamin and zinc. Semi-skimmed milk may be introduced from 2 years providing that your child eats well, has a varied diet and is growing well. Do not give skimmed milk to a child under 5 because of the reduced levels of fat-soluble vitamins A and D. Thereafter skimmed milk is only advisable if your child has a weight problem.

Soya milks may be given if you are following a vegan diet or if your child has a lactose intolerance provided that they are fortified with calcium, vitamin D and vitamin B12. Some may also have sugar added so do consult your doctor or health visitor before giving to your child.

Be wary of fruit squashes and fizzy drinks as these generally contain large amounts of sugar. 'Low sugar', 'no added sugar' and diet varieties that do not contain sugar are widely available but these are sweetened with a sugar substitute such as aspartane. If consumed in sufficiently large quantities this additive can increase a child's thirst and act as a brain stimulant, resulting in behavioural problems. Always read the product label and opt for drinks with minimum additives. Avoid giving tea or coffee to young children too, as the phytic acid present reduces the absorption of iron from other foods.

Encourage older babies to drink from a beaker or feeder cup and gradually cut down on using a bottle. When your baby readily takes drinks from a beaker or cup, phase out the bottle altogether, only offering a bottle at night or when your baby is very tired. Progress from a feeding beaker to a plastic beaker or cup as soon as your child feels confident to do so.

SHOULD CHILDREN SNACK?

Snacks can play a useful role in your toddler's diet providing they are not of the 'empty calorie' crisp and biscuit variety. As any parent knows, young children are extremely active yet they often have quite small appetites. A child's protein and energy requirements are high in relation to their size, and it is sometimes difficult to meet these dietary needs from just three main meals a day. Healthy snacks – that are not laden with sugar or salt – can make up the difference. Keep snacks small, to ensure that your child has room for their main meals. Choose from the following suggestions:

• carrot or cucumber sticks
• whole or sliced fresh fruit, or a little dried fruit
• bread sticks, rice cakes, toast fingers
• mini sandwiches made with peanut butter, cream cheese, hummus, nut, seed or fruit spread
• mini hot cross bun, cheese scone, wholemeal roll
• diced cheese
• wedges of hard-boiled egg
• mini fromage frais
• Fruit Smoothie (see page 108, illustrated above).

Baby Recipes

5–6 Month babies

Now that your baby has been happily eating solid foods for 3–4 weeks, you can begin to increase the number of meals offered and gradually up the amounts, depending on your baby's appetite. Single foods no longer require sieving, but still need to be finely puréed. Simple food blends of two or more ingredients may also be introduced, along with small amounts of lentils and green vegetables, and a wider range of fruits such as papaya, avocado and melon. Stronger flavours should be mixed with potato or rice so they are not overpowering for your baby.

ROOT VEGETABLE HARVEST

4–5 portions (5–6 months)

175 g (6 oz) parsnip, peeled and diced
125 g (4 oz) carrot, peeled and diced
200–250 ml (7–8 fl oz) formula milk or boiled water

Rinse the vegetables and put into a small pan with 150 ml (¼ pint) of the milk or water. Cover and simmer for 15 minutes or until the vegetables are very tender. Purée in a blender with the remaining milk or water, then press through a sieve.

Serve one portion immediately, cool the rest and freeze in an ice cube tray.

SWEET POTATO & APPLE

4–5 portions (5–6 months)

1 sweet potato, about 200 g (7 oz), peeled and diced
1 sweet dessert apple, such as Gala, peeled, cored and diced
175–200 ml (6–7 fl oz) formula milk or boiled water

Rinse the sweet potato and put into a small saucepan with the apple and 150 ml (¼ pint) of the milk or water. Cover and simmer for 12–15 minutes until the sweet potato is tender. Purée the mixture in a blender with the remaining milk or water, then press through a sieve.

Serve one portion immediately, cool the remainder and freeze in an ice cube tray.

SQUASH & LENTIL BAKE

4–5 portions (5–6 months)

125 g (4 oz) butternut squash, peeled
and diced

25 g (1 oz) red lentils, well washed

175–200 ml (6–7 fl oz) boiled water

1 teaspoon sunflower oil

Rinse the butternut squash and put into a small saucepan with the lentils and 150 ml (¼ pint) of the water. Cover and simmer for 30 minutes until the lentils are very soft. Purée in a blender with the remaining water and the oil until smooth, then press through a sieve.

Serve one portion immediately, cool the remainder and freeze in an ice cube tray.

APPLE & PEAR DUET

3–4 portions (5–6 months)

1 sweet dessert apple, such as a Gala

1 ripe pear

3 tablespoons boiled water

Peel, core and roughly chop the apple and pear. Put all the ingredients into a small pan, cover and simmer for 10 minutes until very soft, then press through a sieve.

Serve one portion immediately, cool the remainder and freeze in an ice cube tray.

APRICOT & MILLET FOOL

2–3 portions (5–6 months)

2 tablespoons millet flakes

3 small apricots, well washed, stoned
and chopped

200 ml (7 fl oz) formula milk or water
(approximately)

Put all of the ingredients into a small saucepan and slowly bring to the boil. Cook, stirring constantly, for 4–5 minutes until thickened and the apricots are soft. Purée in a blender, then press through a sieve to remove the apricot skins.

Serve one portion immediately, cool the remainder and freeze in an ice cube tray. As the mixture thickens on cooling, you may need to thin it with a little extra milk or water before serving.

6–9 Month babies

At this stage, food becomes more interesting and varied as your baby's digestive system develops. You can start to introduce gluten-based cereals, such as wheat, barley and oats, plus pasta and flour. Small amounts of tofu, mild yogurts and cheeses – such as cream cheese, ricotta and mild Cheddar – can be incorporated gradually, and cow's milk or soya milk may now be used for cooking. Meals still need to be puréed or finely mashed but most will no longer require sieving.

2 small parsnips, about 300 g (10 oz),
peeled, diced and rinsed
50 g (2 oz) tofu, drained and crumbled
1 tablespoon fresh orange juice
100–150 ml (3½ fl oz–¼ pint) full-fat milk

• Store the remaining tofu from the pack in a small bowl, covered with fresh water. Use within 2 days.
• Rinse the parsnips before cooking to remove any soil residues after peeling.
• As a variation, use a mixture of carrot and parsnip.

CREAMED PARSNIP & TOFU

Blended with mashed parsnip, tofu takes on a mild creaminess and makes a simple supper that is packed with protein. Give your baby small amounts of tofu early on – he is more likely be receptive at this stage than if he first tastes it as an older child. **2 servings (6–9 months)**

Put the parsnips in the top of a steamer, cover and cook over boiling water for 10 minutes until just soft.

Transfer the parsnips to a blender or food processor and add the tofu and orange juice. Blend until smooth, gradually mixing in enough milk to make a smooth thick purée. Adjust the thickness as your baby matures.

Serve half as a baby meal now; cover and chill the other portion and use within 24 hours; or freeze for another meal. Add a little extra water or milk before serving if needed.

BONUS POINTS
• Tofu is one of the few sources of plant protein that supplies all of the essential amino acids.
• The small amount of fresh orange juice aids the absorption of calcium from parsnips, and iron from tofu.
• As the purée is very slightly sweet, it's a good meal to tempt a baby who seems to have lost his appetite.

FOR OLDER BABIES AND TODDLERS
• Mash the parsnips and tofu more coarsely and increase the orange juice slightly for a stronger flavour. Serve with finger foods or stir-fried mixed vegetables for extra crunch.

BABY SPINACH DHAL

Attractively speckled with finely chopped spinach, this dhal is mildly spiced to suit very young tastebuds. Red lentils are less fibrous than other varieties, so they are a good way to introduce a little fibre into your baby's diet.
2 servings (6–9 months)

40 g (1½ oz) red lentils, rinsed

25 g (1 oz) long-grain white rice

1 teaspoon sunflower oil

pinch of ground coriander

pinch of ground turmeric

250 ml (8 fl oz) homemade vegetable stock (see below) or water

25 g (1 oz) frozen chopped spinach, just defrosted, or fresh spinach (prepared weight)

1 fresh tomato, skinned, deseeded and finely chopped

Put the lentils, rice, oil, spices and stock or water into a saucepan and bring to the boil. Cover and simmer for 25 minutes or until the lentils are soft, stirring occasionally and topping up with extra water or stock if needed.

Stir in the spinach and chopped tomato and cook for 2 minutes. Blend to a smooth thick purée, adjusting the texture as your baby matures.

Serve half as a baby meal now; cover and chill the remainder for another meal, using within 24 hours.

BONUS POINTS
• Combining lentils with rice supplies all the essential amino acids your baby needs in one meal.
• Adding tomato at the end of cooking boosts vitamin C levels, which helps to maximize the absorption of calcium and iron from the lentils and spinach.
• Red lentils introduce a little fibre into your baby's diet.

FOR OLDER BABIES AND TODDLERS
• As your baby's tastes become more adventurous you may like to add a little finely crushed garlic or a little fried diced onion.
• If serving to toddlers, up the amount of spice slightly, reduce the amount of liquid and cook the rice separately.

Homemade stock
For babies, make up a batch of your own vegetable stock and freeze in small plastic containers or an ice cube tray. Or save the water used for cooking vegetables and use instead, providing you haven't added salt. Stock cubes must not be used because they contain salt and flavour concentrates.
• To make vegetable stock, chop 1 onion, 3 carrots, 3 sticks of celery, ½ small well washed leek and ½ red pepper or courgette. Fry, stirring, in 2 teaspoons olive oil for 5 minutes, until softened but not browned. Add 1.5 litres (2½ pints) cold water and a small bunch of fresh herbs or a bouquet garni. Bring to the boil and simmer, uncovered, for 30 minutes until reduced slightly. Leave to cool, then strain. Measure the amount needed now; freeze the rest.

• If fresh spinach is used, the extra baby dinner can be frozen.
• Tomatoes can cause an allergic reaction in a few children, so watch your baby closely the first time you include them in the diet.

CARROT & RED PEPPER AMBROSIA

Quick and easy to make, this brightly coloured purée is bound to attract your baby's attention. **2 servings (6–9 months)**

1 carrot, about 125 g (4 oz), peeled and finely diced

¼ red pepper, cored, deseeded and finely chopped

25 g (1 oz) risotto rice, rinsed

200 ml (7 fl oz) homemade vegetable stock (see page 38), or water

1 fresh rosemary sprig (optional)

2–3 tablespoons full-fat cow's milk, or fortified soya milk

Put the carrot, red pepper, rice and stock or water into a saucepan. Add the rosemary if using. Bring to the boil, partially cover the pan and simmer for 15 minutes, or until the rice is tender and most of the liquid is absorbed. Discard the rosemary.

Purée the vegetables and rice with enough milk to make a smooth thick purée, adjusting the texture as your baby matures.

Serve half as a baby meal now; cover and chill the other portion and use within 24 hours; or freeze for another meal. Add a little extra water or milk before reheating if needed.

BONUS POINTS
• The more vibrant a vegetable, the more beta-carotene present – and there are few purées more vivid than this one! Our bodies convert beta-carotene into vitamin A, which is essential for eye function, immunity, growth and cell maintenance.
• White rice is low in fibre so it is an ideal weaning food. Don't be tempted to introduce brown rice yet – your baby's digestive system is still relatively immature and unable to cope with a high fibre intake.

FOR OLDER BABIES AND TODDLERS
• Adjust the consistency to a coarser purée as your baby matures, moving on to a mashed or chopped texture as your baby approaches his first birthday.
• Encourage your child to take an active part in the meal by offering a second spoon for your baby to play with.
• For toddlers, there is no need to purée the mixture. Serve accompanied by warmed bread for extra texture.

• As the rice grains swell on standing, you may need to add a little extra water or milk to loosen the consistency before serving.
• If you haven't any risotto rice, use long-grain white rice instead. Alternatively, substitute quinoa, adjusting the cooking time and topping up with extra stock or water as needed.
• If liked, stir in a little grated Cheddar cheese or finely chopped hard-boiled egg – to boost protein levels, or if your baby didn't eat much at his last meal.

CREAMY VEGETABLE PASTA

Once you can begin to cook pasta for your baby, it won't seem long before he or she is joining in all family meals. Here, broccoli and green beans boost nutrient levels, and cream cheese melts to make a creamy sauce.
2 servings (6–9 months)

40 g (1½ oz) tagliatelle, macaroni or small
    pasta shapes
50 g (2 oz) broccoli, cut into small florets
25 g (1 oz) green beans, sliced
3 tablespoons full-fat cream cheese
few fresh basil leaves (optional)
3–5 tablespoons full-fat milk

Cook the pasta in a pan of boiling water for 6–8 minutes or until tender. Meanwhile, steam the broccoli florets and green beans over boiling water for 5 minutes until tender.

Drain the cooked pasta and place in a blender or food processor with the vegetables, cream cheese and basil, if using. Blend, adding enough milk to make a smooth purée.

Serve half as a baby meal now; cover and chill the other portion and use within 24 hours; or freeze for another meal.

BONUS POINTS
• Broccoli is one of the few vegetables liked by most children. Rich in vitamin C, it is also a useful source of beta-carotene, folate, iron and potassium. Broccoli also contains beneficial phytochemicals that may help to protect against cancer.

FOR OLDER BABIES AND TODDLERS
• Finely chop rather than purée the mixture for older babies, and flavour with a little garlic and extra freshly chopped herbs.
• You can use ready flavoured garlic and herb cream cheese for over-ones.

• Like rice, pasta swells as it stands so you may need to stir a little extra milk into the second pasta meal before serving to your baby.
• If using a microwave to reheat baby food, stir the food thoroughly to disperse any hot spots and always test the temperature of your baby's food before serving.

PUMPKIN PILAF

For this baby pilaf, millet grains take the place of the more traditional rice. They are cooked with pumpkin and lightly flavoured with allspice. When pumpkins are out of season, you can substitute butternut squash.
2 servings (6–9 months)

40 g (1½ oz) millet grain, rinsed
125 g (4 oz) pumpkin, peeled, deseeded and diced
1 tablespoon raisins (optional)
pinch of ground allspice
1 small bay leaf
300 ml (½ pint) homemade vegetable stock (see page 38), or water

Put all of the ingredients into a saucepan and bring to the boil. Cover and simmer for 20–25 minutes until the millet is soft, topping up with extra stock or water as needed. Discard the bay leaf.

Purée the mixture in a blender or food processor to a smooth thick purée, adjusting the texture as your baby matures.

Serve half as a baby meal now; cover and chill the other portion and use within 24 hours; or freeze for another meal.

BONUS POINTS
• A gluten-free cereal, millet provides a good source of energy, protein, B vitamins and minerals. This grain also contains silicon, needed for healthy bones, teeth, nails and hair. Millet is available as whole grains that are used like rice or couscous, and as flakes to make porridge.
• As you would expect from the vivid colour of pumpkin flesh, it is a good source of beta-carotene, which the body converts to vitamin A; it also provides vitamin E. Pumpkin is easily digested and therefore makes an ideal food for young babies.

FOR OLDER BABIES AND TODDLERS
• For babies of 9–12 months, add 2 tablespoons ground almonds with the other ingredients (unless allergy is a consideration). Adjust the texture, making the pilaf slightly coarser. Serve with cooked broccoli florets and warmed strips of Arab bread or pitta bread as finger foods.
• For toddlers, add a little finely chopped fried onion and mushrooms and don't blend the pilaf.

• Millet flakes can be used instead of grains, but you will need to reduce the cooking time to just 5 minutes and stir the mixture frequently as it thickens.

BABY CAULIFLOWER CHEESE

There's no need to go to the trouble of preparing a cheese sauce for your baby – simply purée all of the ingredients together for a deliciously mild cheesy supper that's very quick to make. **2 servings (6–9 months)**

1 small potato, about 150 g (5 oz), peeled, diced and rinsed

150 g (5 oz) cauliflower, cut into small florets, core discarded

2.5 cm (1 inch) piece leek, well rinsed and thinly sliced

40 g (1½ oz) mild Cheddar cheese, grated

75–125 ml (3–4 fl oz) full-fat cow's milk

Put the potato in a steamer over boiling water, cover and cook for 10 minutes. Add the cauliflower and leek and cook for a further 5 minutes until the vegetables are just tender.

Transfer the steamed vegetables to a blender or food processor, add the cheese and blend together, gradually adding enough milk to make a smooth thick purée. (For older babies you are unlikely to need all of the milk.) Alternatively mash the ingredients together, making sure there are no lumps at this stage.

Serve half as a baby meal now; cover and chill the other portion and use within 24 hours; or freeze for another meal.

BONUS POINTS
• Adding milk and cheese to baby meals is a good way to include plenty of protein and calcium in the diet, especially if your baby doesn't seem to be drinking as much milk. A 40 g (1½ oz) portion of Cheddar cheese is equivalent to 200 ml (⅓ pint) of milk.

FOR OLDER BABIES AND TODDLERS
• Adjust the texture of this meal as your baby matures, because it is important for him to become accustomed to slightly coarser foods. Potato and cauliflower are quite soft after cooking so this is an ideal recipe for a first introduction to mashed food.
• For older children, serve with cooked or raw carrot sticks as finger foods.

• Cauliflower can be a little strong for a baby, but mixing it with potato mellows the flavour.
• As a variation, use broccoli instead of cauliflower.
• If you haven't any leek, try adding a few finely chopped chives instead.

PLUM CHEESECAKE

Plums are puréed and mixed with creamy Italian ricotta cheese to make a nutritious pudding. For optimum sweetness, prepare in quantity when fresh plums are plentiful and ripe – and freeze portions for future use.

2–3 servings (6–9 months)

2 large ripe plums, about 200 g (7 oz), washed, stoned and roughly chopped

pinch of ground cinnamon (optional)

3 tablespoons ricotta cheese

Put the plums in a small saucepan with 1 tablespoon water, and the pinch of cinnamon, if using. Cover and cook gently for 5 minutes until soft. Leave to cool.

Spoon the plums and ricotta into a blender or food processor and blend until smooth. Press through a sieve to remove the skins.

Serve a third or half as a baby meal now; cover and chill the rest and use within 24 hours; or freeze for another occasion.

BONUS POINTS
• Plums contain vitamin E, an antioxidant that helps to protect cells from damage. They are also a good source of potassium.
• Combining plums with soft cheese boosts protein and calcium levels.

FOR OLDER BABIES AND TODDLERS
• For extra texture, finely chop rather than purée fruits and mix with the cheese.
• For toddlers and older children, serve the purée as a sauce over sliced bananas or scoops of ice cream.

• Choose organic fruits if possible, as pesticides can be difficult to remove even with careful washing.
• If the plums are slightly sharp, sweeten them with a little mashed banana rather than add sugar.
• Full-fat cream cheese can be used in place of ricotta.
• This is an ideal dessert to freeze in baby portions, and freezing does not significantly affect the nutritional quality or flavour.

PEACH & APPLE FOOL

This creamy smooth fruit fool is naturally sweet, with just a hint of cardamom. Adults and older children can enjoy it as a sauce spooned over sliced peaches and ice cream. For optimum flavour, use ripe peaches and naturally sweet dessert apples, such as Gala. **2 servings (6–9 months)**

1 peach, rinsed, halved, stoned and roughly chopped

1 dessert apple, rinsed, quartered, cored and roughly chopped

2 cardamom pods, bruised (optional)

2 tablespoons natural bio yogurt

Put the peach and apple into a small saucepan with 1 tablespoon water, and the cardamom pods, if using. Cover and simmer gently for 5 minutes until the fruit is tender. Take out the cardamom pods and discard.

Purée the fruit in a blender or food processor until smooth, then press through a sieve to remove the fruit skins and cardamom seeds. Cover and leave to cool, then mix the purée with the yogurt.

Serve half as a baby meal now; cover and chill the other portion and use within 24 hours; or freeze for another meal.

• As the quantity of fruit is small, you may prefer to simply press the fruits through a sieve into a bowl, rather than use a blender.

BONUS POINTS
• Rich in vitamin C, this pudding will boost the absorption of iron if it follows an iron-rich main course.
• Some bought fruit yogurts contain a surprising amount of sugar. By making your own desserts, it's easy to omit sugar and ensure your baby's food is free from additives.

FOR TODDLERS AND OLDER CHILDREN
• Serve as a sauce over scoops of vanilla ice cream and extra sliced fruits.
• Alternatively, freeze the purée in lolly moulds for a healthy treat.

9–12 Month babies

By now your baby will be used to a varied and interesting diet. Over the next few months he or she will be eating nearly all the same foods as the rest of the family, albeit finely chopped or coarsely mashed. Sharing family meals will become a much more regular occurrence and your baby will soon begin to feed himself – an exciting time for everyone!

1 small potato, about 125 g (4 oz), peeled and diced

1 small carrot, about 125 g (4 oz), peeled and diced

125 g (4 oz) butternut squash, peeled and diced

50 g (2 oz) broccoli, cut into small florets, stems sliced

4 teaspoons sunflower seeds

1 teaspoon sunflower oil

2–3 tablespoons full-fat cow's milk, or fortified soya milk

> • If possible, buy organically grown vegetables for your family's meals.

MIXED VEGETABLE PLATTER

This veggie feast is given a protein boost with the addition of a smooth sunflower seed paste that tastes so mild, your baby won't notice it. Vary the mix of vegetables according to what you have in your fridge: parsnips, green beans, red pepper, courgettes and spinach are all suitable.
2 servings (9–12 months)

Rinse the potato, carrot and squash, drain and put into a steamer set over a saucepan of simmering water. Cover and steam for 10 minutes. Add the broccoli, re-cover the pan and cook for a further 5 minutes.

Meanwhile grind the sunflower seeds to a smooth paste with the oil and 1 tablespoon of the milk in a food processor spice mill attachment, or a well washed coffee grinder. Alternatively, pound the seeds using a pestle and mortar, gradually adding the oil and milk.

Mash or chop the vegetables, mixing in the sunflower seed paste and enough milk to give the required consistency. Adjust the texture as your baby matures.

Serve half as a baby meal now; cover and chill the remainder and use within 24 hours; or freeze for another meal.

BONUS POINTS
• Sunflower seeds contain protein, B group vitamins and calcium.

FOR TODDLERS AND OLDER CHILDREN
• Serve with extra cooked or raw vegetable sticks or strips of toast as finger foods. Provided there isn't a family history of nut or other allergies, you can substitute cashew nuts or hazelnuts for sunflower seeds to make a nut paste.

LENTIL HOTPOT

Now that your baby is getting older, you can flavour plain lentils by adding onion fried in a little oil, or a little garlic for adventurous tastebuds.

2 servings (9–12 months)

1 teaspoon sunflower oil

2 tablespoons finely chopped onion

1 carrot, about 125 g (4 oz), rinsed and diced

1 small potato, about 150 g (5 oz), rinsed and diced

½ garlic clove, crushed (optional)

40 g (1½ oz) red lentils, rinsed

200 ml (7 fl oz) homemade vegetable stock (see page 38), or water

2 tablespoons fresh orange juice

1 tablespoon finely chopped fresh chives

Heat the oil in a medium saucepan, add the onion and fry for 4–5 minutes until lightly browned. Add the carrot, potato and garlic, if using, then stir in the lentils and stock or water. Bring to the boil, cover and simmer for 25 minutes, topping up with a little extra stock or water if needed.

Stir the orange juice and herbs into the lentil mixture, then mash or chop to suit your baby.

Serve half as a baby meal now; cover and chill the remainder and use within 24 hours; or freeze for another meal.

BONUS POINT
• The addition of a little orange juice provides vitamin C which aids the absorption of iron from the lentils.

FOR TODDLERS AND OLDER CHILDREN
• There is no need to mash or chop – simply serve the lentil mixture in bowls with steamed broccoli florets or green beans.

• Red lentils are a good storecupboard standby as they don't require soaking or lengthy cooking like other dried pulses.
• If you have fresh herbs in the garden, use a mixture in the hotpot – perhaps a little finely chopped tarragon and parsley, or sage and chives.
• Freeze baby dinner in a clearly labelled small plastic container or sealed plastic bag. Use within 6 weeks.

MEDITERRANEAN VEGETABLES WITH QUINOA

If you haven't used the grain quinoa before, now is the time to do so! It is a South American alternative to rice or couscous, and a superior source of vegetable protein. You can buy quinoa from most healthfood shops.

2 servings (9–12 months)

1 teaspoon sunflower oil

1 tablespoon finely chopped onion

½ red pepper, cored, deseeded and finely chopped

½ orange pepper, cored, deseeded and finely chopped

½ medium courgette, about 75 g (3 oz), finely chopped

½ garlic clove, finely crushed (optional)

25 g (1 oz) quinoa, rinsed well

½ teaspoon tomato purée

300 ml (½ pint) homemade vegetable stock (see page 38), or water

1 tomato, skinned, deseeded and finely chopped

2 teaspoons finely chopped fresh oregano, marjoram or basil (optional)

Heat the oil in a medium saucepan, add the onion and fry for 4–5 minutes until lightly browned. Add the peppers, courgette, and garlic, if using, and fry for 3 minutes.

Stir in the quinoa, tomato purée and stock or water. Bring to the boil, then lower the heat, cover the pan and simmer for 20 minutes or until the quinoa grains are soft. Add the chopped tomato, and chopped herbs, if using. Cook, uncovered, for 3 minutes.

Mash or chop the mixture to the required texture for your baby. Spoon half into a bowl and serve now. Cover and chill the other portion and use within 24 hours; or freeze for another meal.

BONUS POINTS
• Quinoa is the only grain that provides all of the essential amino acids, making it an excellent source of protein for vegetarians. It is also rich in iron and calcium.
• Adding the tomato at the end of cooking adds vitamin C and helps to boost iron and calcium absorption.

FOR TODDLERS AND OLDER CHILDREN
• There is no need to mash or chop the food. Simply serve in a bowl with warm bread.

• Rice, bulgar wheat or millet grains are suitable alternatives to quinoa.
• Fresh herbs impart fragrance and flavour to dishes. If you do not have a garden, try growing a selection of herbs in pots on a balcony, or in window boxes.

CHEESY POLENTA WITH COURGETTES

As your baby's feeding progresses, preparing meals is less time-consuming, because you no longer need to purée or mash food. Instead you can simply chop it finely, using a knife and fork. Serving soft polenta with a chunkier chopped vegetable sauce is a good halfway meal to encourage your baby towards foods with more texture. **1 serving (9–12 months)**

1 teaspoon olive oil

50 g (2 oz) courgette, rinsed and finely diced

1 mushroom, rinsed and finely chopped

1 tomato, skinned, deseeded and finely chopped

½ teaspoon tomato purée

25 g (1 oz) quick-cook polenta

25 g (1 oz) mild Cheddar cheese, grated

Heat the oil in a small saucepan, add the courgette and mushroom and fry, stirring, for 2–3 minutes until very lightly browned. Add the tomato, tomato purée and 3 tablespoons water. Cover and cook for 5 minutes.

Bring 100 ml (3½ fl oz) water to the boil in another small saucepan. Sprinkle in the polenta in a steady stream, stirring. Cook over a medium heat for 1–2 minutes, stirring constantly until thickened.

Stir in the cheese and spoon into a serving bowl. Mash the vegetable sauce if required. Spoon the sauce on top of the polenta and cool slightly before serving.

BONUS POINTS

• Polenta, or coarsely ground cornmeal, provides energy in the form of carbohydrate, protein and minerals, such as iron and potassium. It is a gluten-free grain, suitable for young babies and anyone with gluten intolerance, but check pack labels – some manufacturers coat polenta grains in flour during processing.

• Young children need fat as a concentrated form of energy. The best sources are those foods that are rich in other nutrients too. Cheese, for example, provides fat, but it is also rich in protein, calcium and the fat-soluble vitamins A, D, E and K.

FOR OTHER AGE GROUPS

• For younger babies, mash or purée the vegetable sauce and stir into the polenta.

• For older children, don't mash the vegetables – simply spoon the sauce alongside the polenta.

• If preferred, mash the vegetables and stir into the soft polenta.

• Finely chopped red or orange pepper, or butternut squash can be mixed with the courgette or used in its place.

• For adventurous babies, add a little finely chopped rosemary or basil to the vegetable sauce.

BROCCOLI & FENNEL RISOTTO

This light, fresh-tasting one-pot supper, with just a hint of lemon, is quick and easy to put together. **2 servings (9–12 months)**

1 teaspoon olive oil

50 g (2 oz) piece of fennel bulb, rinsed and finely chopped

50 g (2 oz) risotto rice, rinsed

300–350 ml (10–12 fl oz) hot homemade vegetable stock (see page 38), or water

1 free-range egg

75 g (3 oz) broccoli florets, rinsed and cut into tiny florets, stems chopped

1 tablespoon lemon juice

• 1 tablespoon finely chopped onion or 2 tablespoons finely chopped leek can be used instead of fennel.

• The risotto may be frozen, without the egg, for up to 6 weeks.

Heat the oil in a medium saucepan, add the fennel and fry for 2–3 minutes until softened. Stir in the rice and cook for 1 minute. Add three-quarters of the stock and bring to the boil. Simmer gently, uncovered, for 10 minutes, stirring occasionally.

Meanwhile, add the egg to a separate pan of boiling water and cook for 8 minutes to hard-boil. Drain and immerse in cold water; set aside.

Add the broccoli to the rice and moisten with the remaining stock or water if needed. Cook for 5 minutes, stirring more frequently towards the end of cooking as the liquid is absorbed. Stir in the lemon juice.

Spoon half of the risotto into a bowl. Mash or chop if required. Peel and finely chop half of the egg and sprinkle over the baby dinner.

Wrap the remaining egg half in cling film; cover the other portion of risotto. Refrigerate and use within 24 hours.

BONUS POINTS
• A risotto base is a good way to introduce your baby to more interesting vegetables and new vegetable combinations.
• Broccoli is rich in vitamin C and beta-carotene, and contains some folate, iron and potassium.
• Omit the egg if following a vegan diet. Boost protein supplies by adding finely chopped tofu, or ground toasted hazelnut butter, or a sprinkling of ground almonds.

FOR OTHER AGE GROUPS
• For younger babies, omit the egg. Mash or purée the risotto, adding a little extra stock, water or milk. For babies over 6 months, you can add a little of the chopped egg yolk.
• For older children, cut the broccoli and fennel into larger pieces.

CHEAT'S CARROT CASSOULET

Forget about long slow cooking in the oven, this speedy cassoulet – made with canned haricot beans, carrots and parsnips – is cooked on the hob.
2 servings (9–12 months)

1 carrot, about 125 g (4 oz), peeled, diced and rinsed

1 small parsnip, about 150 g (5 oz), peeled, diced and rinsed

2.5 cm (1 inch) piece green leek, well rinsed and thinly sliced

50 g (2 oz) canned haricot beans (without salt or sugar), well rinsed

few fresh herb sprigs, such as sage, rosemary and marjoram

150 ml (¼ pint) homemade vegetable stock (see page 38), or water

1 tomato, skinned, deseeded and finely chopped

Put the carrot, parsnip, leek, haricot beans and herb sprigs into a medium saucepan. Add the stock or water and bring to the boil, then cover the pan. Lower the heat and simmer for 15 minutes until the vegetables are tender, topping up with extra stock if needed.

Add the tomato and cook for a further 2–3 minutes until softened, then discard the herb sprigs. Mash or chop the cassoulet for your baby.

Serve half as a baby meal now; cover and chill the remainder and use within 24 hours; or freeze for another meal.

BONUS POINTS
• Pulses are a good source of protein, minerals, B vitamins and fibre. This recipe is a good way to introduce high fibre pulses into your child's diet in small amounts so that you don't overload tiny tummies.

FOR TODDLERS AND OLDER CHILDREN
• There is no need to mash or chop the cassoulet. Simply serve in bowls, accompanied by warm bread.

• Buy canned beans without added salt or sugar. These are usually organic and sometimes sold in a different part of the supermarket from other canned pulses. Home-cooked dried beans can be used instead if preferred.
• Vary the fresh herbs according to what you have in the garden or refrigerator salad drawer.
• Add a little crushed garlic if liked.

MINI APPLE CUSTARD POTS

Naturally sweetened with a little poached apple, these small baked custards are made with basic ingredients from the larder, fridge and fruit bowl.
2 servings (9–12 months)

1 dessert apple, peeled, cored and
  chopped
pinch of ground cinnamon
1 egg
150 ml (¼ pint) full-fat milk

Put the apple into a small saucepan with 1 tablespoon water and the cinnamon. Cover and cook gently for 5 minutes until the apple is soft.

Butter 2 ramekins or other small heatproof dishes and divide the poached apple between them.

Lightly beat the egg in a bowl. Heat the milk in a pan until almost boiling, then gradually beat into the egg. Strain the custard over the poached apple in the ramekins.

Stand the ramekins in a small roasting tin and surround with boiling water to come halfway up the sides of the dishes. Bake in a preheated oven at 180°C (350°F) Gas Mark 4 for 20–25 minutes until the custard is set and feels quite firm to the touch. If it is at all wobbly, return to the oven for a further 5 minutes.

Allow to cool before serving. Use the second portion within 24 hours. (The custards are not suitable for freezing.)

BONUS POINTS
• Eggs are a good source of protein, and an important source of vitamin B12 for vegetarians. They are also rich in minerals, including iron and zinc.
• The vitamin C from the apple aids the absorption of calcium from the milk.

FOR TODDLERS AND OLDER CHILDREN
• This pudding is popular with older children. It is also delicious served with a little sieved blackberry purée or a spoonful of low-sugar blackberry jam.

• As a variation, replace the apple with 1 small banana, mashed and mixed with 1 teaspoon of cocoa powder.
• Make sure eggs are well cooked when serving to young children. Look out for the Lion mark on free-range organic eggs, which denotes that the eggs are from hens vaccinated against salmonella and produced by farmers following the RSPCA'S Freedom Food Initiative.

PRUNE & BANANA SUNDAE

If you have a small hand-held electric baby blender, you can whizz up this delicious, naturally sweet dessert in seconds. It is so quick that you can prepare a single portion as you need it. **1 serving (9–12 months)**

3 ready-to-eat stoned prunes, about
   25 g (1 oz)
1 tablespoon fresh orange juice
½ small banana, sliced
2 tablespoons natural bio yogurt

Blend the prunes and orange juice together until finely chopped. Add the banana and yogurt and blend briefly, then spoon into a small bowl and serve.

BONUS POINTS
• Bananas are a good source of energy. They are also rich in potassium which is needed to help regulate the blood.
• Prunes are similarly rich in potassium and also contain vitamin B6, iron and fibre. Like bananas, they provide a concentrated form of energy.
• Prune juice is low in fibre, but can help to alleviate constipation.

FOR TODDLERS AND OLDER CHILDREN
• Toss chopped prunes in orange juice, then layer in plastic tumblers or serving dishes, with sliced banana and yogurt.
• Encourage children to snack on dried fruits such as prunes, peaches and apricots rather than biscuits or crisps, and add to packed lunchboxes.

• Do not prepare this dessert in advance, as the banana would discolour.
• If you do not have an electric blender, chop the prunes very finely and mix with the orange juice, then stir in mashed banana, followed by the yogurt.

ORCHARD FRUIT COMPOTE

This very simple, warm fresh fruit salad makes the most of late summer fruits and tastes wonderful topped with a spoonful of mild, creamy-tasting natural bio yogurt. Vary the fruits according to what you have in the fruit bowl, and add a few diced ready-to-eat dried apricots or dates if you like.
2 servings (9–12 months)

1 ripe plum, rinsed, stoned and chopped
1 ripe peach, peeled, stoned and chopped
1 ripe pear, peeled, cored and chopped
4 teaspoons natural bio yogurt

Put all of the fruits in a small saucepan with 1 tablespoon water. Cover and simmer for 5 minutes. Allow to cool slightly.

Spoon half of the warm compote into a small bowl and top with a little yogurt to serve. Cover the remaining fruit salad, chill and use within 24 hours; or freeze for another time.

BONUS POINT
• These fruits are naturally sweet when ripe, so there is no need to add sugar to the compote. You should avoid adding sugar to foods for under-ones except when cooking very sharp fruits such as gooseberries and rhubarb.

FOR OTHER AGE GROUPS
• For younger children, purée and sieve fruits and serve on their own or mixed with a little natural bio yogurt.
• For older children, you may like to serve the warm fruit with a scoop of just melting vanilla ice cream.

• If your choice of fresh fruit is limited, add 2–3 diced ready-to-eat dried apricots or dates, or some canned apricots in natural juice.
• Adjust the texture to suit your baby; mash or purée if preferred. Some babies take longer to adjust to coarser textures than others.

OTHER IDEAS
Vitamin C is needed daily. If you haven't time to make a pudding, offer your baby some prepared fruit as finger food, or fruit purée. Try the following:
• Kiwi fruit is a particularly good source of vitamin C. Either cut the kiwi into wedges or serve with the top cut off and a small teaspoon, so that your child can eat it 'boiled egg' style.
• Papaya is easy to digest and a lovely treat for your baby. Halve lengthways, then scrape out the black seeds from the centre. Remove the skin, then slice, chop or mash the flesh to a cream.
• Melon is often popular with babies. Peel and remove all the seeds, then slice, chop or purée the flesh for younger babies.

PUMPKIN & ROSEMARY BREAD STICKS

Homemade bread sticks are ideal finger food for older babies. Keep a supply of these handy in the freezer and take out a few at a time as you need them. They will defrost in about 30 minutes at room temperature, and are perfect for teething babies to munch on. **Makes 60 (9–12 months)**

4 tablespoons pumpkin seeds

4 tablespoons olive oil

750 g (1½ lb) strong white bread flour

7 g (¼ oz) sachet easy-blend dried yeast

2 tender stems of fresh rosemary, leaves
very finely chopped

500 ml (17 fl oz) warm water
(approximately)

Add the pumpkin seeds to a heated small heavy-based frying pan and toss over a medium heat for about 1 minute until lightly toasted. Grind the toasted seeds with 2 tablespoons of the oil to a smooth paste in a clean spice or coffee grinder, or using a pestle and mortar.

Put the flour into a bowl, add the pumpkin seed paste, yeast and rosemary, then mix in enough water to form a soft but not sticky dough. Knead vigorously on a well floured surface, then cut the dough into 60 pieces. Roll each piece into a rope, about 20 cm (8 inches) long.

Lay the dough sticks on 2 large oiled baking trays, spacing them slightly apart. Brush lightly with the remaining olive oil and cover loosely with clingfilm. Leave to prove in a warm place for about 20 minutes or until well risen. Remove the clingfilm.

Bake the bread sticks in a preheated oven at 220°C (425°F) Gas Mark 7 for 8–10 minutes, transposing the trays after 5 minutes to ensure even cooking. Transfer to wire racks to cool.

Put a few bread sticks in an airtight container and use within 24 hours. Pack the rest into freezer bags or one large plastic container, seal and freeze for up to 6 weeks; take out a few at a time as required.

BONUS POINTS
• It is much better to encourage children to snack on savoury foods rather than sweet ones. Even babies of 9 months and over will find comfort chewing on these bread sticks – especially if they are troubled with teething.
• Pumpkin seeds are a good source of iron and phosphorus; they also contain smaller amounts of potassium, magnesium and zinc. As the seeds are finely ground in these bread sticks, the texture isn't a problem for babies.

FOR TODDLERS AND OLDER CHILDREN
• Serve bread sticks with carrot sticks and hummus or yogurt-based dips for a more filling snack.

• Use half white and half wholemeal flour if preferred.
• Omit the pumpkin seeds if you prefer, or if there is a family history of allergies. Plain dough sticks are just as popular with children.

SAVOURY SWIZZLE STICKS

These savouries are also ideal for adult drinks parties. You can make them with homemade shortcrust pastry if you prefer. **Makes 40 (9–12 months)**

425 g (14 oz) pack of 2 ready-rolled frozen puff pastry sheets, defrosted
1 egg
1 teaspoon low-sodium yeast extract
2 teaspoons low-salt/low-sugar tomato ketchup

Unroll the pastry sheets and cut into 1 cm x 7.5 cm (½ inch x 3 inch) strips. Mix the egg, yeast extract and tomato ketchup together and brush over the pastry.

Take one strip and press one end on to a greased baking sheet. Twist the pastry strip to give a corkscrew effect, then press the other end on to the baking sheet to secure in place. Repeat with the remaining pastry strips, spacing them slightly apart on 2 baking sheets.

Bake in a preheated oven at 200°C (400°F) Gas Mark 6 for 8–10 minutes until well risen and golden. Loosen the strips while still warm, then leave to cool completely on the baking sheets.

Store in a plastic box and use within 2 days; or freeze for up to 6 weeks.

• As low-sodium yeast extract is strong tasting, use it sparingly – especially for young children.

FOR TODDLERS AND OLDER CHILDREN
• Serve as an accompaniment to soups or add to lunchboxes.

CHEESE STRAWS

Ever popular, these are a healthier snack than crisps or biscuits – especially if you serve them with raw vegetable sticks. **Makes 50 (9–12 months)**

125 g (4 oz) plain white flour
50 g (2 oz) butter, diced
75 g (3 oz) mild Cheddar cheese, grated
1 egg yolk
1 egg, beaten

Put the flour into a bowl, add the butter and rub in using the fingertips (or an electric mixer) until the mixture resembles fine breadcrumbs. Stir in the cheese, then the egg yolk mixed with 1 tablespoon beaten egg to bind the dough.

Knead lightly on a floured surface, then roll out to the thickness of a £1 coin. Cut into 1 cm x 5 cm (½ inch x 2 inch) strips. Brush with the remaining beaten egg, separate the straws and place, slightly apart, on a baking sheet.

Bake in a preheated oven at 200°C (400°F) Gas Mark 6 for 8–10 minutes until golden. Leave to cool on the baking sheets.

Pack in a plastic box and use within 3 days; or freeze for up to 6 weeks.

• Use half white, half wholemeal flour if preferred.

FOR TODDLERS AND OLDER CHILDREN
• Add to children's packed lunchboxes. Serve at parties instead of crisps.

Home & hungry

The recipes in this chapter can be made in advance and finished off quickly when needed.

COWBOY BEANS

Saucy beans:

175 g (6 oz) dried pinto, borlotti or cannellini beans, soaked in cold water overnight

1 bay leaf

1 tablespoon olive oil

1 onion, finely chopped

1 garlic clove, crushed

1 tablespoon plain flour

1 teaspoon paprika

300 ml (½ pint) vegetable stock

1 tablespoon tomato purée

1 tablespoon brown sugar

1 teaspoon Dijon mustard (optional)

salt and black pepper (optional)

Slaw:

1 small banana, sliced

1 small orange, peeled and segmented

1 small dessert apple, cored and diced

75 g (3 oz) red cabbage, cored and finely shredded

3 tablespoons sprouted alfalfa seeds, rinsed

> • Freeze beans in portions, without the slaw topping, for up to 6 weeks.

Serves 4

Drain the beans, rinse with cold water, then put into a saucepan with the bay leaf. Cover with plenty of fresh cold water. Bring to the boil and boil rapidly for 10 minutes. Skim off any scum from the surface and simmer for 1 hour or until tender.

Heat the olive oil in a frying pan, add the onion and garlic and fry for 5 minutes, stirring until golden. Stir in the flour and paprika and cook for 1 minute, then stir in the stock, tomato purée, sugar and mustard, if using. Season lightly if required.

Drain the cooked beans, return to the saucepan and stir in the sauce. Cover and set aside.

When ready to serve, bring to the boil, cover and simmer for 15 minutes. Meanwhile, toss all the slaw ingredients together in a bowl. Spoon the beans into serving bowls, top with the slaw and serve with warm bread.

BONUS POINTS

• Making your own saucy beans has the advantage that you know exactly what's in them. Standard canned baked beans are high in sugar and salt.

• Sprouting seeds are like mini powerhouses – packed with nutrients. They're also fun to grow on trays lined with wetted kitchen paper, on a windowsill.

• This recipe is ideal for children on a dairy-free or vegan diet.

OKAY FOR UNDER-ONES?

5–9 months Not suitable. See pages 10–11 and 35–44 for other ideas.

9–12 months Mash plain boiled beans with some boiled potato and carrot and flavour with a little tomato purée, fresh, skinned, deseeded *tomatoes* or a little crushed garlic.

CHEESY PUMPKIN SAUSAGES

Win your children's non-vegetarian friends round with these tasty meat-free sausages. The pumpkin isn't obvious, but it makes the sausages deliciously light and moist. Most children love ketchup with sausages, but do look for a brand that is comparatively low in salt and sugar. **Serves 4**

2–3 tablespoons sunflower oil

50 g (2 oz) hazelnuts

25 g (1 oz) butter or margarine

1 small onion, finely chopped

150 g (5 oz) peeled, deseeded pumpkin (prepared weight), coarsely grated

150 g (5 oz) Cheddar cheese, grated

175 g (6 oz) fresh white breadcrumbs

2 free-range eggs, separated

150 g (5 oz) broccoli, cut into florets

150 g (5 oz) mixed frozen peas and sweetcorn

salt and black pepper (optional)

Heat 1 teaspoon sunflower oil in a frying pan, add the hazelnuts and fry for 2–3 minutes until golden, shaking the pan constantly. Remove from the pan and chop finely.

Heat the butter or margarine in the frying pan, add the onion and fry, stirring, for 4–5 minutes, until softened and lightly browned. Stir in the pumpkin and cook for 2 minutes. Take the pan off the heat and stir in the cheese, 75 g (3 oz) of the breadcrumbs, the egg yolks, chopped hazelnuts and a little seasoning, if liked.

Lightly beat the egg whites in a shallow dish with a fork. Divide the sausage mixture into 8 portions and shape into small sausages. Dip in the egg white, then roll in the remaining breadcrumbs to coat completely.

Heat the remaining oil in the cleaned frying pan, add the sausages and fry for 4–5 minutes, turning several times, until golden.

Meanwhile cook the broccoli and frozen vegetables in a small pan of boiling water for 3 minutes. Drain and spoon on to plates. Add the sausages and serve with a little tomato ketchup if liked.

BONUS POINTS

• Recent research suggests that hazelnuts are one of our best 'brain foods'. However, if allergy is a consideration, you should omit the nuts from the sausages.

• If your child is reluctant to drink milk, you can boost calcium levels with cheese in cooking. A 25 g (1 oz) piece of Cheddar or similar hard cheese provides the same amount of calcium as a 140 g (4½ oz) pot of yogurt or 200 ml (⅓ pint) of full-fat milk.

OKAY FOR UNDER-ONES?

Not suitable. See pages 10–12 and 35–55 for other suggestions.

• Vary the cheeses if you like – Wensleydale and Caerphilly also work well – but look for the vegetarian symbol which denotes that the cheese is made with animal-free rennet.

• Carrot can be used instead of pumpkin.

• These sausages freeze well. Open freeze for 2 hours, then pack into a plastic box and freeze up to 6 weeks. Defrost for 1 hour at room temperature before cooking.

VEGGIE PUFF PIE

Although there isn't any cream in this tasty leek and mushroom filling, finely ground cashew nuts add a lovely richness to the sauce. Get the children to help you decorate the pie top – adding pastry numerals or their initials.
Serves 4

100 g (3½ oz) cashew nuts

3 tablespoons olive oil

1 leek, about 250 g (8 oz), thinly sliced

250 g (8 oz) button mushrooms, quartered

1 tablespoon plain flour

450 ml (¾ pint) full-fat milk

375 g (12 oz) ready-made puff pastry (fresh or frozen and defrosted)

beaten egg, to glaze

salt and black pepper (optional)

Scatter the cashew nuts over the bottom of a grill pan and toast briefly under a hot grill, turning frequently, until golden. Turn into a blender, add 2 tablespoons of the oil and work to a smooth paste.

Heat the remaining oil in a frying pan, add the leek and mushrooms and fry, stirring, for 3–4 minutes until lightly browned. Stir in the flour, then add the nut paste and gradually mix in the milk. Bring to the boil, stirring. Season lightly if liked. Spoon into a 1.2 litre (2 pint) pie dish.

Roll out the pastry on a lightly floured surface until 5 cm (2 inches) larger all round than the top of the pie dish. Cut off a 1 cm (½ inch) wide strip of pastry from around the edge. Moisten the rim of the pie dish with a little water and position the pastry strip on the rim. Brush with beaten egg, then lift the pastry lid into position.

Press the pastry edges together well, trim off excess and stamp out shapes or numerals using small biscuit cutters. Brush the top of the pie with egg, add the pastry decorations and brush these with egg. Cover loosely with clingfilm and set aside until ready to cook.

Bake the pie in a preheated oven at 200°C (400°F) Gas Mark 6 for about 20 minutes until well risen and golden. Serve with carrots and broccoli.

BONUS POINT
• Cashew nuts are an excellent source of protein for vegetarians, but they should be avoided for children under 3 years of age if there is any family history of asthma, eczema or peanut allergy. If allergy isn't likely to be a problem, most health experts agree that ground nuts may be introduced when a child is 9–12 months old.

OKAY FOR UNDER-ONES?
Not suitable. See pages 10–12 and 35–55 for other ideas.

• Try using hazelnuts or almonds instead of cashews.

• If you intend to freeze this pie, use chilled (rather than frozen) pastry and freeze before baking. Defrost overnight in the refrigerator and bake as above.

LENTIL THATCH

This inexpensive supper is comforting, warming and popular with children of all ages. Serve without the decorative finish if you prefer, or make up your own design – perhaps a cat with carrot whiskers and a cherry tomato nose.
Serves 4

1 tablespoon sunflower oil

1 onion, finely chopped

2 carrots, about 175 g (6 oz), diced

2 celery sticks, sliced

1 garlic clove, crushed

100 g (3½ oz) red lentils, rinsed

900 ml (1½ pints) vegetable stock

2 teaspoons tomato purée

625 g (1¼ lb) baking potatoes, peeled
      and cut into chunks

3 tablespoons full-fat milk

40 g (1½ oz) butter or margarine

salt and black pepper (optional)

To finish (optional):

2 carrots, sliced lengthways

1 red pepper, cored and deseeded

4 frozen peas, defrosted

• Some margarines contain fish oils and unexpected animal products. Read labels carefully and look for the vegetarian symbol 🄥.
• These individual cottage pies freeze well and are a good standby for days when you haven't the time or energy to cook. Wrap well in freezer film or foil, seal in freezer bags and freeze for up to 6 weeks.

Heat the oil in a saucepan, add the onion and fry for 4–5 minutes until lightly browned. Add the carrots, celery and garlic, cook for 1 minute, then stir in the lentils, stock and tomato purée. Bring to the boil and simmer uncovered, stirring occasionally, for 30 minutes or until the lentils are soft.

Meanwhile cook the potatoes in a separate pan of boiling water for 15 minutes or until tender. Drain and mash with the milk and half of the butter or margarine. Season lightly if liked.

Season the lentils lightly and spoon into four 300 ml (½ pint) ovenproof square dishes. Top with the mashed potato and cover loosely with foil.

When ready to serve, dot with the remaining butter and bake in a preheated oven at 200°C (400°F) Gas Mark 6 for 20 minutes until piping hot.

To finish if desired, add raw carrot roof tiles, red pepper windows and door, a pea door knob, and carrot strips to mark the window panes. Serve hot.

BONUS POINTS

• Lentils are high in protein. Unlike pulses, they do not need soaking before cooking.
• Carrots are a useful source of zinc, especially for children on a vegan diet. Although zinc is present in small amounts, the contribution is valuable as children happily eat generous portions of this vegetable.
• This recipe is suitable for children on a dairy-free or vegan diet if you use soya milk in the mash, and vegetable margarine rather than butter. Brush the potato topping with a little oil before baking.

OKAY FOR UNDER-ONES?

5–6 months Not suitable. Instead, cook potato and carrot in the minimum amount of water, with the celery in a steamer above. Purée with formula milk or homemade vegetable stock.
6–9 months Use homemade stock and omit the raw vegetable decoration. Blend in a food processor or blender to the desired texture.
9–12 months Use homemade stock and chop the vegetables very finely or mash before serving if preferred.

TODDLERS' TAGINE

Although this recipe includes a few spices, the finished dish has a mild, mellow flavour. Serve with quinoa, or couscous if you prefer. **Serves 4**

1 tablespoon olive oil

1 small onion, finely chopped

1 garlic clove, crushed

375 g (12 oz) baby new potatoes, halved

2 carrots, about 175 g (6 oz), cut into chunks

½ teaspoon paprika

large pinch of ground allspice

large pinch of ground cinnamon

400 g (13 oz) can chopped tomatoes

200 g (7 oz) can baked beans

125 g (4 oz) quinoa or couscous

175 g (6 oz) broccoli, cut into small florets

salt and black pepper

Heat the oil in a saucepan, add the onion and fry for 4–5 minutes, stirring occasionally, until lightly browned. Stir in the garlic, potatoes, carrots and spices; cook for 1 minute.

Add the tomatoes, baked beans and a little seasoning. Bring to the boil, cover and simmer for 25 minutes. Set aside until ready to serve.

If using quinoa, add to a pan half-filled with boiling water and simmer for 15 minutes or until tender. If using couscous, put into a bowl, pour on 250 ml (8 fl oz) boiling water and leave to soak for 5–10 minutes until softened; fork through the grains to fluff up.

Steam the broccoli for 5 minutes or until just tender. Reheat the tagine on the hob for 5 minutes until piping hot. Spoon the quinoa or couscous on to serving plates and top with the tagine and broccoli.

BONUS POINT
• Quinoa is a highly nutritious grain – rich in protein, iron and calcium. It is a particularly good source of protein as it is the only grain that contains all of the essential amino acids.

OKAY FOR UNDER-ONES?
5–9 months Not suitable. Instead, make up a simple smooth purée with potato and carrot cooked in a little formula milk or homemade stock, adjusting the texture as your baby gets older.
9–12 months Use homemade vegetable stock in place of the tomatoes and baked beans and mash or purée some of the tagine, serving broccoli florets as finger food.

• You can use canned *chickpeas* or butter beans (preferably without added salt or sugar) in place of baked beans. Top up the sauce with a little vegetable stock if necessary.
• Freeze individual portions in small plastic containers or sealed bags for up to 6 weeks.

VEGETABLE & BARLEY STEW WITH DUMPLINGS

This is the ideal dish to come home to on a cold winter's day – give everyone spoons and forks to scoop up all the tasty gravy. Make the dumplings really small so that they cook quickly. **Serves 4**

1 tablespoon sunflower oil

1 onion, finely chopped

2 carrots, about 175 g (6 oz), chopped

1 small parsnip, 150 g (5 oz), chopped

200 g (7 oz) swede, chopped

75 g (3 oz) pot barley

1.2 litres (2 pints) vegetable stock

2 tablespoons malt extract

2 tablespoons chopped fresh sage, or
   ½ teaspoon dried

100 g (3½ oz) frozen peas, cooked and
   drained

Dumplings:

125 g (4 oz) self-raising flour

50 g (2 oz) vegetable suet

2 tablespoons chopped fresh parsley

4–5 tablespoons cold water

salt and black pepper (optional)

To finish (optional):

chopped fresh parsley

> • If preferred, simmer the stew, covered, on the hob for 45 minutes, stirring occasionally and topping up with extra stock as needed.
> • Freeze stew without dumplings in handy portions for up to 6 weeks.

Heat the oil in a flameproof casserole (or use a frying pan and transfer the stew to a casserole before cooking in the oven). Add the onion and fry, stirring occasionally, for 4–5 minutes until lightly browned.

Add the root vegetables, barley, 900 ml (1½ pints) of the stock, the malt extract and sage. Bring to the boil. Cover and cook in a preheated oven at 180°C (350°F) Gas Mark 4 for 1 hour. Set aside until required.

Shortly before serving, make the dumplings. Mix the flour, suet and parsley in a bowl with a little seasoning. Add enough water to mix to a soft, slightly sticky dough. Gently roll into 12 small balls with floured hands.

Add the remaining stock to the stew and bring to the boil on the hob. Season lightly if required, add the dumplings and re-cover. Simmer on the hob for 10–12 minutes until the dumplings are well risen and fluffy, then sprinkle in the peas. Serve in bowls, topped with a little chopped parsley if liked.

BONUS POINTS

• Pot barley is nutritious and thought to have anti-viral properties. Look for it in healthfood shops but don't confuse it with pearl barley which has most of the bran and germ removed along with some of the protein, vitamins and minerals.

• Malt extract is a good source of phosphorus for healthy bones, and magnesium which is vital for nerve and muscle function. Derived from barley grains, it is naturally sweet and adds depth and flavour to slow-cooked stews, cakes and bakes.

OKAY FOR UNDER-ONES?

5–6 months Not suitable. Instead, make a smooth purée with carrot, swede and potato cooked in water or formula milk.

6–9 months Not suitable because of the high fibre content of barley. Instead make a purée from the vegetables above, cooking in cow's milk or water and blending to the desired texture.

9–12 months Mash or purée the stew and serve without the dumplings.

CLEOPATRA'S RICE

Based on an everyday Egyptian favourite, this cheap supper dish combines lentils with rice for optimum protein. Topped with colourful courgette sticks and spoonfuls of creamy bio yogurt, it is delicious served with warm pitta bread. **Serves 4**

125 g (4 oz) green lentils, rinsed

1.2 litres (2 pints) vegetable stock

1 teaspoon ground cumin

1 teaspoon ground coriander

1 bay leaf

150 g (5 oz) basmati rice, rinsed

2 tablespoons sunflower oil

1 onion, finely chopped

1 garlic clove, crushed (optional)

4 teaspoons tahini (optional)

grated rind and juice of 1 lemon

2 courgettes, about 250 g (8 oz), cut into sticks

1 teaspoon clear honey (optional)

150 g (5 oz) natural bio yogurt

1 tablespoon chopped fresh mint (optional)

Put the lentils, 1 litre (1¾ pints) of the stock, the spices and bay leaf into a large saucepan. Bring to the boil, then cover and simmer for 30–40 minutes or until tender, stirring occasionally.

Cook the rice separately in boiling water until tender, then drain and rinse with hot water.

Heat 1 tablespoon of the oil in a frying pan. Add the onion and garlic, if using, and fry until golden.

Pour off excess stock from the lentils and reserve. Add the fried onion, rice, tahini, if using, lemon rind and juice to the lentils. Cover and set aside until ready to serve.

Heat the remaining oil in the cleaned frying pan. Add the courgette sticks and stir-fry for 5 minutes until lightly browned. Drizzle with the honey, if using, and cook for 1 minute.

Reheat the lentils, stirring, and moisten with the reserved stock if needed. Pile into serving bowls. If preferred flavour the yogurt with the chopped mint. Spoon the yogurt on top of the lentil mixture and surround with the courgette sticks. Serve with warmed pitta breads.

BONUS POINTS

• Bio yogurt is much milder and creamier tasting than other natural yogurts, making it more popular with children. The active bacteria in bio yogurt is also thought to help prevent tummy upsets.

• Adding lemon juice at the end of cooking helps to boost vitamin C levels and aids the absorption of calcium from tahini and yogurt.

• You can freeze this dish (without the courgettes or yogurt) in individual portions in small plastic containers or plastic bags for up to 6 weeks. Reheat in the microwave, but remember to stir well to ensure there are no hot spots.

OKAY FOR UNDER-ONES?

5–6 months Not suitable. See pages 10–11 and 35–6 for other ideas.

6–9 months Omit the lemon rind, juice, honey and fried onions. Mash or purée more rice than lentils with a little yogurt and steamed courgette, mixing to the desired texture with extra milk.

9–12 months Omit the honey and fried onions. Mash or coarsely purée rice and lentils with a little lemon juice, yogurt, mint and steamed courgette.

RED PEPPER & POLENTA BAKE

Bright, colourful and very moreish, this bake appeals to young tastebuds, and polenta makes a pleasant change from potatoes, rice or pasta. If your children like aubergine, try using it in place of the butternut squash. **Serves 4**

500 ml (17 fl oz) water
125 g (4 oz) instant polenta
125 g (4 oz) medium Cheddar cheese, grated
25 g (1 oz) butter
5 teaspoons olive oil
1 onion, finely chopped
1 red pepper, cored, deseeded and cut into large squares
375 g (12 oz) butternut squash, deseeded, peeled and cut into large cubes
1 garlic clove, crushed
400 g (13 oz) can chopped tomatoes
150 ml (¼ pint) vegetable stock
2 teaspoons finely chopped fresh rosemary (optional)
salt and black pepper

Bring the 500 ml (17 fl oz) water to the boil in a saucepan. Add the polenta in a steady stream, stirring all the time. Cook, stirring continuously, until the polenta is very thick and smooth. Take off the heat.

Reserve a little cheese for the topping. Stir the rest into the polenta with the butter and a little seasoning. Spoon into an oiled shallow rectangular tin or dish, approximately 18 x 28 x 4 cm (7 x 11 x 1½ inches). Leave to cool and set.

Heat 3 teaspoons of the oil in a saucepan, add the onion and fry, stirring, for 4–5 minutes until lightly browned. Add the red pepper, squash and garlic and fry for 2 minutes. Stir in the tomatoes, stock, rosemary, if using, and a little seasoning if liked. Cover and simmer for 15 minutes. Spoon into a 2 litre (3½ pint) shallow ovenproof dish.

Loosen the polenta and turn out on to a chopping board. Stamp out hearts, stars or circles using biscuit cutters. Arrange the polenta shapes over the top of the pepper mixture, brush with the remaining oil and sprinkle with cheese. Cover loosely with clingfilm and refrigerate until needed.

When ready to serve, remove the clingfilm and bake in a preheated oven at 200°C (400°F) Gas Mark 6 for 15 minutes. Serve with steamed green beans.

BONUS POINTS
• Packed with vitamin C and beta-carotene, the plant form of vitamin A, these vegetables will boost your child's immune system and eye function.
• Suitable for children on a vegan or dairy-free diet if you omit the cheese from the polenta and replace the butter with vegetable margarine.
• Suitable for children on a gluten-free diet, but do check the polenta pack carefully. Some manufacturers coat polenta grains with flour during processing.

OKAY FOR UNDER-ONES?
5–6 months Not suitable. Instead, give a smooth purée of steamed butternut squash.
6–9 months Add homemade stock or water to the pepper mixture. Purée with some polenta, adding extra water if needed to obtain the desired texture.
9–12 months Finely chop the pepper mixture and stir into soft (just cooked) polenta with a little mild grated cheese if liked.

• You can freeze this recipe in a freezerproof baking dish before the final baking, covered with clingfilm and sealed in a freezer bag, for up to 6 weeks.

BEAN & PESTO POTS

A delicious main meal soup-cum-stew, served with tiny savoury scones. Buy canned beans without added salt and sugar, cook your own, or use small pasta shapes instead of beans if you prefer. **Serves 4**

1 tablespoon olive oil
1 small onion, finely chopped
1 carrot, about 125 g (4 oz), diced
2 celery sticks, about 40 g (1½ oz), sliced
1 garlic clove, crushed
100 g (3½ oz) cooked or drained canned
    cannellini beans
750 ml (1¼ pints) vegetable stock
2 teaspoons tomato purée
salt and black pepper

Cheese and almond scones:

200 g (7 oz) self-raising flour
50 g (2 oz) butter or block margarine
50 g (2 oz) ground almonds
125 g (4 oz) Cheddar cheese, grated
1 free-range egg, beaten
150 ml (¼ pint) full-fat milk (approximately)

To finish soup:

75 g (3 oz) green beans, sliced
3 tablespoons frozen peas
3 tomatoes, about 150 g (5 oz), skinned,
    deseeded and chopped
1–2 teaspoons pesto (optional)

• For nut-free scones, replace the ground almonds with an extra 25 g (1 oz) self-raising flour.
• Freeze scones in bags, and soup in portion packs for up to 6 weeks.

Heat the oil in a saucepan, add the onion and fry for 4–5 minutes, stirring occasionally, until lightly browned. Stir in the carrot, celery and garlic and fry for 2 minutes, then add the cannellini beans, stock, tomato purée and a little seasoning. Bring to the boil, then lower the heat and simmer for 20 minutes.

Meanwhile, make the scones. Put the flour into a bowl, add the butter in pieces and rub in with your fingertips (or use an electric mixer) until the mixture resembles fine crumbs. Stir in the ground almonds, then the cheese. Add half of the egg and mix in enough milk to make a smooth, soft dough.

Lightly knead the dough, then gently roll out to a 1.5 cm (¾ inch) thickness. Stamp out rounds or hearts with a 5 cm (2 inch) cutter and place on a lightly greased baking sheet. Re-roll and cut more scones from trimmings. Brush the tops with beaten egg. Bake in a preheated oven at 200°C (400°F) Gas Mark 6 for 10–12 minutes until well risen and golden.

Put a lid on the soup pan and cover the scones with a clean tea towel. Set aside until ready to serve.

Warm the scones in the oven at 180°C (350°F) Gas Mark 4 for 5 minutes or microwave, two at a time, for 30 seconds on high. Add the green beans, peas and tomatoes to the soup and simmer for 5 minutes.

Ladle the 'soup' into bowls and stir in pesto, if using, to taste. Serve with the warm buttered scones.

BONUS POINT

• A good way to encourage your children to eat a range of vegetables and pulses. If they are going through an 'anti-veg' stage, try keeping a star chart and award a star for every fruit or vegetable eaten each day – working towards a special treat.

OKAY FOR UNDER-ONES?

4–6 months Not suitable. See pages 10–11 and 35–6 for other ideas.
6–9 months Use homemade stock, and pasta instead of the beans; omit the pesto and scones. Purée with enough stock to give the desired texture.
9–12 months Use homemade stock. Mash vegetables and beans to desired texture, and flavour with a tiny amount of pesto. Serve with toast fingers.

LENTIL BOLOGNESE

This is an ideal meal for your children to share with non-vegetarian friends. Cook their favourite pasta shape, or spaghetti if they enjoy twirling it and you don't mind the mess! **Serves 4**

75 g (3 oz) Puy lentils, rinsed

1 tablespoon olive oil

1 onion, finely chopped

1 garlic clove, crushed

2 small carrots, diced

2 small courgettes, diced

50 g (2 oz) button mushrooms, sliced

400 g (13 oz) can chopped tomatoes

150 ml (¼ pint) vegetable stock

2 tablespoons tomato purée

3 tablespoons chopped fresh marjoram, or ¾ teaspoon dried

200 g (7 oz) pasta spirals

grated Cheddar or Parmesan cheese, to serve

salt and black pepper

Put the lentils into a saucepan, add plenty of cold water to cover and bring to the boil. Lower the heat and simmer, uncovered, for 30 minutes or until tender. Drain and reserve.

Heat the oil in a saucepan, add the onion, garlic and carrots and fry for 4–5 minutes, stirring occasionally, until lightly browned. Add the courgettes and mushrooms and cook for 2 minutes. Stir in the tomatoes, stock, tomato purée, marjoram and a little seasoning.

Bring to the boil, cover and simmer for 5 minutes, stirring occasionally. Stir in the drained lentils, cover and set aside until required.

When ready to serve, cook the pasta in a saucepan of boiling water until al dente – tender but firm to the bite. Meanwhile, reheat the bolognese sauce for 5 minutes, stirring well. Drain the pasta, toss with the sauce and spoon into bowls. Sprinkle with a little cheese to serve.

BONUS POINTS

• Lentils are a good source of protein, and eating them in combination with pasta – another source of vegetable protein – supplies all of the essential amino acids that our bodies need.

• Carrots are an excellent source of beta-carotene, the plant form of vitamin A and an important antioxidant that may help to protect cells from damage.

OKAY FOR UNDER-ONES?

4–6 months Not suitable. See pages 10–11 and 35–6 for other ideas.

6–9 months Use homemade stock. As lentils are high in fibre and tomatoes are quite acidic, use these sparingly. Instead, include more vegetables and pasta, adding a little mild grated Cheddar. Purée with enough milk to give the desired texture.

9–12 months Cook the lentils until very soft. Drain, mash, then mix in small quantities with finely chopped pasta or tiny soup pasta.

• For those children on a vegan or dairy-free diet make sure that the pasta is egg-free and omit the cheese.

• Freeze the bolognese in handy portions in plastic bags for up to 6 weeks. Defrost overnight in the refrigerator or by microwave, stirring well to ensure there are no hot spots. Serve with pasta.

Fast high teas

Rustling up a quick tea for your hungry children that is packed with protein, vitamins and minerals – and meets with their approval – can be tricky, especially if any of them are going through a fussy stage. These perfect solutions are mostly designed for two mini diners but can be easily doubled up to serve larger families or visiting friends.

IPPY DIPPERS

Try this oven-baked version of egg and chips for a healthy, fuss-free supper that children will love. **Serves 2**

1 baking potato, about 250 g (8 oz), scrubbed
½ parsnip, about 150 g (5 oz), peeled
2 small carrots, about 150 g (5 oz), peeled
3 tablespoons olive oil
pinch of turmeric
pinch of paprika
2 free-range eggs

Cut the potato and parsnip into wedge-shaped chips, about 6 cm (2½ inches) long. Cut the carrots into thick sticks, about the same length. Cook in a pan of boiling water for 4 minutes. Meanwhile, heat the oil in a small roasting tin in the oven at 220°C (425°F) Gas Mark 7 for 2 minutes.

Drain the vegetables, add to the hot oil and toss to coat. Sprinkle with the spices and roast in the oven for 20 minutes. Turn the vegetables and make a space in the middle of them. Break the eggs into this space and bake for a further 5 minutes until the eggs are well cooked.

Transfer to serving plates and serve with tomato ketchup.

BONUS POINTS
• A concentrated source of protein, eggs also provides vitamin B12 which is essential for the nervous system but can be difficult for vegetarians to obtain.
• Leaving the skin on the potato ensures that valuable vitamins and minerals found just beneath the skin are not lost.

OKAY FOR UNDER-ONES?
4 months Not suitable. Instead, simmer potato with parsnip or carrot in formula milk, then purée and sieve until smooth.
5–6 months Cook all the root vegetables in milk as above, then purée.
6–9 months Cook the root vegetables in full-fat cow's milk and purée with well cooked egg yolk to the desired texture.
9–12 months Finely chop the vegetables and whole egg. Or let children pick up cooled vegetable chips and serve finely chopped egg from a spoon.

• Conservative children may prefer this dish without the parsnip.
• For adventurous tastebuds, add sweet potato and butternut squash.
• Or for a Mediterranean version, make 'ippy dippers' from thick sliced courgettes, aubergine, peppers and mushrooms. Flavour with chopped garlic rather than spices.

BEAN & FETA FALAFEL

Traditionally made with dried chickpeas, these little spicy patties are popular with young and old alike. Here they are made with frozen broad beans for speed, and mixed with a little chopped feta for added flavour. I serve them in mini 'party' pitta breads – the perfect size for tiny hands to hold – with a dollop of minted or plain yogurt. Alternatively, you could serve them with tomato ketchup. **Serves 2–3**

150 g (5 oz) frozen baby broad beans

½ small onion, roughly chopped

½ teaspoon ground cumin

1 teaspoon ground coriander

2 tablespoons chopped fresh parsley (optional)

50 g (2 oz) feta cheese, well drained, chopped

1 tablespoon plain flour

2 tablespoons sunflower oil

6 mini pitta breads

1 Little Gem lettuce, roughly torn

3 tablespoons natural bio yogurt

little finely chopped fresh mint (optional)

¼ cucumber, sliced

1 dessert apple, cored and sliced

Add the broad beans to a pan of boiling water, bring back to the boil and simmer for 4 minutes; drain.

Put the beans into a food processor with the onion, spices, parsley, if using, and feta; process until finely chopped. Or finely chop all the ingredients by hand and mix in a bowl.

Divide the mixture into 6 portions, then press into small oval patties between well floured hands. Heat the oil in a frying pan and fry the falafel for 5 minutes, turning several times until golden.

Meanwhile, warm the pitta breads in the oven or under the grill, according to pack directions.

Split the pitta breads open, pop a little lettuce and a falafel into each one, then spoon in a little plain yogurt, or yogurt flavoured with chopped mint. Serve with cucumber and apple slices.

BONUS POINTS
• Serving falafel in pittas combines the proteins in the beans and bread to give a better balance of essential amino acids.
• Broad beans contain beta-carotene which the body converts to vitamin A, plus some iron, phosphorus, niacin, and vitamins C and E, as well as protein and soluble fibre.

OKAY FOR UNDER-ONES?
4–6 months Not suitable. See pages 10–11 and 35–6 for other ideas.
6–9 months As broad beans are high in fibre only give small amounts to your baby – puréed with other vegetables such potato, carrot or parsnip. Reduce the spices and blend in a dessertspoonful of mild grated cheese, or sieved ricotta or cottage cheese.
9–12 months Finely chop or process the broad beans with a tiny piece of onion and a pinch each of cumin and coriander. Mix to the desired texture with milk and serve with strips of warmed pitta bread.

• For vegans, omit the feta and yogurt and serve with tomato sauce made with fresh or canned tomatoes, flavoured with a little garlic and chopped fresh coriander.
• If you can't get mini pittas, use halved standard pitta breads.

KIDS' KEDGEREE

An Anglo-Indian rice dish, kedgeree was popular back in Victorian times. This vegetarian version uses easy-cook brown rice mildly flavoured with Indian spices. It is flecked with peas, sweetcorn and chopped watercress, and served topped with wedges of hard-boiled egg. **Serves 2**

2 teaspoons sunflower oil

½ small onion, finely chopped

75 g (3 oz) easy-cook brown rice, rinsed

1 bay leaf

large pinch of turmeric

½ teaspoon ground coriander

450 ml (¾ pint) vegetable stock

2 free-range eggs

75 g (3 oz) frozen mixed peas and
   sweetcorn

3 tablespoons chopped watercress
   leaves

3 tablespoons single cream

Heat the oil in a saucepan, add the onion and fry, stirring occasionally, for 4–5 minutes until lightly browned. Stir in the rice and cook for 1 minute, then add the bay leaf, spices and stock. Bring to the boil, then simmer uncovered, stirring occasionally, for 20 minutes.

Meanwhile, put the eggs in a small pan of water, bring to the boil and simmer for 8 minutes. Rinse with cold water, crack the shells and immerse in cold water until cool enough to handle. Shell the hard-boiled eggs and cut into wedges, or chop into smaller pieces.

Add the frozen vegetables to the rice and cook for 3 minutes. Drain off any excess stock, then stir in the watercress and cream. Spoon on to plates and top with the hard-boiled eggs to serve.

BONUS POINTS
• The starch in brown rice is digested and absorbed slowly, making your child feel full and satisfied for longer.
• Although brown rice contains more vitamins and minerals than white rice, the bran present also contains phytic acid – which inhibits the absorption of iron and calcium. Easy-cook brown rice is a good compromise: during processing the rice is soaked in water, then steamed locking in the nutrients just below the surface of the bran. The outer layer of bran is then milled away producing a brown rice that cooks more quickly and is popular with children.
• Sprinkling chopped watercress into the kedgeree helps to boost iron levels. Increase the body's absorption of this important mineral by serving with food or a drink rich in vitamin C, such as a glass of orange juice.

OKAY FOR UNDER-ONES?
4–6 months Not suitable. See pages 10–11 and 35–6 for other ideas.
6–9 months Reduce spices and add only a few peas and sweetcorn as these are fibrous, and make the amount with diced butternut squash or carrot. Include the hard-boiled egg yolk, but not the white. Purée the rice, vegetables and watercress with milk to the required texture.
9–12 months Mash kedgeree and whole egg with a little milk.

• As a variation, add 50 g (2 oz) broccoli, cut into tiny florets, with the peas and sweetcorn, omitting the watercress.
• Leave out the spices if preferred. For flavour add a crushed small garlic clove with the rice, and a little tomato purée with the stock.

OODLES OF NOODLES

All children seem to love pasta. Here it is topped with a fresh tomato sauce, subtly flavoured with garlic and sun-dried tomato paste. Noodles are tricky for children to eat, but many love the challenge of twiddling them around a fork. For very young children, cook pasta twists or shells instead. **Serves 3**

2 teaspoons olive oil

½ small onion, finely chopped

1 small garlic clove, crushed

4 tomatoes, about 275 g (9 oz), skinned and chopped

½ courgette, about 75 g (3 oz), finely diced

125 g (4 oz) dried tagliatelle

25 g (1 oz) frozen peas

1 teaspoon sun-dried tomato paste

2 tablespoons single cream

To serve:

Parmesan or Cheddar cheese shavings

few fresh basil leaves (optional)

Heat the oil in a saucepan, add the onion and fry, stirring occasionally, for 4–5 minutes until lightly browned. Stir in the garlic, tomatoes and courgette. Cover and cook gently for 10 minutes, stirring occasionally, to make the sauce.

Meanwhile, cook the pasta in a large saucepan of boiling water until al dente – tender but firm to the bite.

Add the peas and tomato paste to the sauce and cook for 3 minutes, then stir in the cream.

Drain the pasta and spoon on to plates. Spoon on the sauce and top with cheese shavings and a few basil leaves, if liked.

BONUS POINTS

• Tomatoes are a good source of carotenoids – red and yellow pigments that are thought to help protect the body from some forms of cancer by neutralising free radicals. Tomatoes also contain useful amounts of vitamin C and E, and are a good source of potassium, which is needed to help regulate blood pressure.

• Suitable for a vegan diet provided you use egg-free pasta, omit the cream from the sauce and don't top with cheese shavings.

OKAY FOR UNDER-ONES?

4–6 months Not suitable. See pages 10–11 and 35–6 for other ideas.

6–9 months Omit the peas. Purée 1 tablespoon of the sauce and 3 tablespoons pasta with a little milk to the required texture. Include a little grated mild Cheddar if liked.

9–12 months Finely chop or mash the food to the desired texture.

• If preferred, omit the courgette or replace with a little finely diced carrot and red pepper.

• A 200 g (7 oz) can of tomatoes could be used instead of fresh ones; break them up with a spoon as the sauce cooks.

• To make cheese shavings, pare fine slices from a piece of cheese with a swivel vegetable peeler.

• To serve 1 child and 2 adults, double the quantities of ingredients.

STRIPY MACARONI CHEESE

Make this quick and easy pasta dish in heatproof glass dishes so that children can see and count the different layers. **Serves 2**

125 g (4 oz) dried macaroni

100 g (3½ oz) broccoli, cut into tiny florets, stems sliced

1 carrot, about 125 g (4 oz), sliced

50 g (2 oz) frozen sweetcorn

15 g (½ oz) butter

15 g (½ oz) plain flour

200 ml (7 fl oz) full-fat milk

1 teaspoon Dijon mustard (optional)

100 g (3½ oz) medium Cheddar cheese, grated

1 tablespoon fresh breadcrumbs

quartered cherry tomatoes, to serve

Cook the macaroni in a pan of boiling water until al dente – tender but firm to the bite. Meanwhile, steam the broccoli, carrot and sweetcorn in a steamer over a separate pan of boiling water for 6–7 minutes. Lift the steamer off the pan; keep covered.

Melt the butter in the dried steamer pan. Stir in the flour and cook for 1 minute, then gradually mix in the milk and bring to the boil, stirring until the sauce is thickened and smooth. Stir in the mustard, if using, and three-quarters of the cheese.

Drain the macaroni and stir into the sauce. Spoon two thirds of the macaroni cheese into two 200 ml (7 fl oz) individual ovenproof dishes. Arrange the carrot, broccoli and sweetcorn in layers on top, then cover with the rest of the macaroni cheese.

Sprinkle with the remaining cheese and breadcrumbs and brown under a hot grill for 5 minutes. Set on serving plates and allow to cool slightly before serving, with cherry tomatoes.

BONUS POINTS

• An easy, interesting way to encourage children to eat a varied selection of vegetables.

• A good source of dairy foods, rich in protein and calcium which is vital for growing bones and teeth. Many children cut down on milk drinks as they get older so it makes sense to include dairy products in cooking.

OKAY FOR UNDER-ONES?

4–6 months Not suitable. Instead, serve a purée made with broccoli, carrot and formula milk or water.

6–9 months Omit the sweetcorn as it is quite fibrous and difficult for a young baby to digest. Purée the mixture with extra milk to the desired texture.

9–12 months Finely chop or mash the food to the required texture.

• For children with very different appetites, vary the sizes of the dishes, or make one to serve both children, using a 450 ml (¾ pint) heatproof glass soufflé or pie dish.

• Toss all of the vegetables into the sauce with the pasta rather than layer them, if preferred.

• As a variation, use 100 g (3½ oz) frozen spinach, defrosted and thoroughly drained, in place of the broccoli; chopped raw tomatoes in place of the carrot; and peas instead of sweetcorn.

CHEESY CLOUDS

These light airy cheese soufflés conceal a surprise layer of broccoli and take only a little longer to make than a basic cauliflower or broccoli cheese. Serve with slices of toast, stamped into moon and star shapes using biscuit cutters. A great dish to offer visiting children. **Serves 4**

150 g (5 oz) broccoli, cut into small florets

40 g (1½ oz) butter

1 tablespoon grated Parmesan cheese

25 g (1 oz) plain flour

150 ml (¼ pint) full-fat milk

100 g (3½ oz) double Gloucester cheese with chives, or medium Cheddar cheese, grated

1 teaspoon Dijon mustard (optional)

pinch of cayenne pepper

3 free-range eggs, separated

To serve:

cherry tomatoes, halved

toast slices

• Pregnant women and young children should not eat softly cooked eggs, so make sure that the soufflé is well risen and cooked right through to the centre.

• Make the surprise layer a mix of steamed broccoli and cauliflower, or cauliflower and sliced leeks, for a change. Or leave out the surprise layer and serve with raw carrot and cucumber sticks.

Steam the broccoli for 3–4 minutes or until just tender. Meanwhile, grease four 200 ml (7 fl oz) individual soufflé dishes with a little of the butter, then sprinkle with the Parmesan.

Melt the remaining butter in a small saucepan, stir in the flour and cook for 1 minute. Gradually stir in the milk and bring to the boil, stirring until thick and smooth.

Take the pan off the heat and stir in the cheese, mustard, if using, and cayenne. Gradually beat in the egg yolks, one at a time.

Whisk the egg whites in a separate bowl until soft, moist peaks form. Stir a little of the egg white into the cheese mixture to lighten it, then carefully fold in the rest.

Divide the broccoli between the prepared dishes, then pour the cheese mixture over the top. Bake in a preheated oven at 190°C (375°F) Gas Mark 5 for 15 minutes. Scoop the soufflés on to individual plates and serve, with cherry tomatoes and warm toast.

BONUS POINTS

• Eggs are a good source of zinc, a mineral which can be difficult to obtain on a vegetarian diet and necessary for growth, sexual development and healing.

• Broccoli is sometimes regarded as 'the king of vegetables', as it is rich in vitamin C and beta-carotene, and contains some folate, iron and potassium. Steam broccoli rather than cook it in water – to preserve its water-soluble vitamin C.

OKAY FOR UNDER-ONES?

4–6 months Not suitable. Instead, simmer broccoli and a little diced potato in formula milk or water and purée until smooth, sieving if necessary.

6–12 months Simmer broccoli in full-fat milk and purée with a little grated Cheddar cheese, adjusting the consistency to suit your baby. A little well cooked egg yolk may be added from 6 months; well cooked whole egg may be added from 9 months.

TOMATO CLOWNS

If your children like pizzas, they are sure to enjoy these baked tomatoes – filled with melting mozzarella and served on a bed of soft polenta. Adding carrot eye lashes is bound to raise a smile and takes only a minute or two.
Serves 2

2 tomatoes

1 teaspoon pesto

4 mini mozzarella cheeses from a 125 g (4 oz) pack, well drained

2 pitted black olives, halved

1 teaspoon olive oil

200 ml (7 fl oz) water

50 g (2 oz) polenta

15 g (½ oz) butter

2 tablespoons full-fat milk

1 small carrot, cut into thin sticks

2 red pepper slices, cut from the base

salt and black pepper

Halve the tomatoes crossways and scoop out the cores and seeds. Turn the tomato halves upside down to drain.

Put the tomatoes, cut side up, in a small heatproof dish. Spoon a tiny amount of pesto into each one, then add a mini mozzarella and an olive half. Drizzle with oil and bake in a preheated oven at 200°C (400°F) Gas Mark 6 for 10 minutes.

When the tomatoes are almost ready, bring the water to the boil in a small nonstick saucepan. Add the polenta in a steady stream, stirring all the time, then cook, stirring constantly, for 2–3 minutes until thickened and smooth. Take off the heat and stir in the butter and milk. Season lightly to taste.

Spoon the soft polenta on to 2 plates. Add the baked tomato eyes and position carrot sticks for eyelashes. Position a small red pepper ring on each face with a sliver of carrot in the centre to resemble a mouth. Serve at once.

BONUS POINT
• Polenta is very finely milled cornmeal and therefore suitable for those on a gluten-free diet, providing the grains have not been coated with flour during processing; do check pack details if this is relevant.

OKAY FOR UNDER-ONES?
4–6 months Not suitable. See pages 10–11 and 35–6 for other ideas.
6–9 months Not suitable. Instead, purée a tiny amount of skinned tomato with plain cooked polenta and mix with a little low-fat cream cheese to the desired texture for your baby.
9–12 months Omit the pesto. Finely chop or process the tomato and cheese, then stir into a little of the polenta.

• In general you should avoid adding salt, but some foods – such as polenta – need a little seasoning otherwise they taste very bland. Discourage children from sprinkling salt on their food at the table, and never add salt to under-ones' food.
• For fussy children omit the pesto from the tomatoes.
• For children on a vegan diet, omit the mozzarella and fill the tomatoes with a finely diced ratatouille mixture. Add dairy-free margarine and extra water to the polenta in place of butter and milk.

CABBAGE CUPS WITH CREAMY CARROT SAUCE

Children love vibrant colours and this bright colourful supper dish will definitely attract their attention. **Serves 2**

150 g (5 oz) carrots, thickly sliced

400 ml (14 fl oz) vegetable stock

50 g (2 oz) couscous

1 tablespoon raisins

2 ready-to-eat dried apricots, chopped

¼ red pepper, deseeded and
  diced

2 tablespoons frozen peas

pinch of ground allspice

2 teaspoons olive oil

2 Savoy cabbage leaves, thick stems
  removed

salt and black pepper

Put the carrots and 300 ml (½ pint) of the stock in the base of a steamer pan and bring to the boil. Cover and simmer for 10 minutes. Meanwhile, put the couscous in a bowl, pour on the remaining hot stock and leave to soak for 5 minutes.

Add the raisins, apricots, red pepper, peas, allspice and oil to the soaked couscous and mix with a fork; season lightly. Spoon the mixture into the cabbage leaves, folding up the sides of the leaves to encase the filling.

Lift the cabbage cups into the steamer above the carrots. Cover and cook for 5 minutes until the cabbage is tender; keep the steamer covered.

Purée the carrots with half of the stock until smooth. Gradually blend in enough of the remaining stock to make a pouring sauce.

Spoon the sauce over the base of 2 serving plates. Place the cabbage parcels on top and serve.

BONUS POINT

• Red peppers are an excellent source of vitamin C. A medium red pepper contains as much vitamin C as 3 oranges!

OKAY FOR UNDER-ONES?

4–6 months Not suitable. See pages 10–11 and 35–6 for other ideas.

6–9 months Use homemade stock. Purée all ingredients together, adding only a small piece of cabbage and extra stock to make a softer consistency.

9–12 months Use homemade stock. Finely chop or mash all of the ingredients together to the required texture.

• Bulgar wheat can be used instead of couscous: soak in stock as above, but for 15 minutes.

• If you do not have any allspice, use a tiny pinch each of ground cinnamon and freshly grated nutmeg instead.

• As a variation, use butternut squash in place of carrot; it makes an equally delicious, vibrant sauce.

VEGETABLE WIGWAMS

This colourful supper dish is quick and easy to assemble. Young children can pick up the vegetables and eat them as finger food, using a spoon for the rice. Tomato ketchup is a popular condiment – opt for a low-sugar brand.
Serves 2

75 g (3 oz) basmati rice

75 g (3 oz) baby corn cobs, halved lengthways

75 g (3 oz) carrot, cut into sticks

50 g (2 oz) green beans, halved

1 teaspoon sunflower oil

1 tablespoon sesame seeds

1 teaspoon light soy sauce

40 g (1½ oz) frozen chopped spinach, defrosted and well drained

50 g (2 oz) fresh tofu, rinsed, drained and cut into small dice

One-third fill a steamer pan with water, bring to the boil and add the rice. Simmer for 5 minutes. Put all of the vegetables into the steamer, place on the pan and steam for 5 minutes or until both rice and vegetables are tender.

Meanwhile, heat the oil in a small frying pan. Add the sesame seeds and fry until lightly browned. Take the pan off the heat and add the soy sauce. Quickly cover the pan and set aside.

Drain the rice, rinse with boiling water and mix with the spinach and tofu. For children under 3 years, grind the sesame seeds until smooth, adding a little extra oil if needed. Add the seeds to the rice.

Spoon the rice into mounds on 2 serving plates. Arrange the vegetables upright around the rice to resemble an Indian's wigwam. Serve with a little tomato ketchup if liked.

BONUS POINTS
• Made from soya beans, tofu is a rare source of high-quality vegetable protein which contains all of the essential amino acids. Firm tofu is available chilled in sealed packs of water or in longlife tetra packs and holds its shape better than softer silken tofu.
• This novel presentation may be just enough to tempt children to eat a healthy variety of vegetables.
• Sesame seeds contain useful amounts of calcium and vitamin E. They add a delicious nutty flavour, especially when mixed with a little soy sauce. Try them sprinkled over the top of mashed parsnips or carrots, too.

OKAY FOR UNDER-ONES?
Omit the soy sauce and sesame seeds for all under-ones.
5 months Finely purée the vegetables, rice and spinach with formula milk or water to a smooth, slightly sloppy purée.
6–9 months Mash or purée rice, vegetables and a small amount of tofu, adding enough milk or water to give the desired texture.
9–12 months Finely chop or mash the rice and vegetables with a little full-fat milk or soya milk.

• Vary the vegetables according to what you have in the fridge or freezer. If your children do not like spinach, simply leave it out.
• Shredded omelette can also be added to the rice instead of the tofu if preferred.

Storecupboard saviours

These recipes are based on items that you will find in the larder, fridge or freezer, and all take the minimum time to prepare – ideal when you haven't pre-planned your children's tea, or you haven't had the time or energy to shop.

BEAT-THE-CLOCK PIZZAS

250 g (8 oz) self-raising flour

50 g (2 oz) butter or block margarine, diced

1 free-range egg

100 ml (3½ fl oz) full-fat milk

4 tablespoons passata

4 teaspoons chopped fresh oregano, marjoram or mixed herbs

50 g (2 oz) frozen sweetcorn

50 g (2 oz) medium Cheddar or mozzarella cheese, grated

To finish:

2 green peppers, halved, cored and deseeded

1 red pepper, halved, cored and deseeded

• To make one large pizza rather than individual ones, shape the dough into a 25 cm (10 inch) circle and bake for 15 minutes.

These scone-based pizzas are simple to make and shape, and they don't need to be left to rise before baking. Use them to introduce your child to the basics of 'telling the time'. Let your child arrange the clock hands on the pizzas – to match those on the kitchen clock. **Makes 4**

Put the flour into a bowl and rub in the butter using your fingertips (or an electric mixer) until the mixture resembles fine crumbs. Stir in the egg and enough milk to mix to a smooth soft, but not sticky dough.

Knead lightly on a floured surface, then divide the dough into 4 pieces. Roll out each one to a 12 cm (5 inch) circle. Place on a large greased baking sheet and brush with passata. Sprinkle with the herbs and sweetcorn.

Top with the grated cheese and bake in a preheated oven at 200°C (400°F) Gas Mark 6 for 10 minutes until well risen and the cheese is melted.

Cut the main clock numerals from green pepper, using tiny number cutters. Cut red pepper clock hands. Arrange on the pizzas and serve warm, with cherry tomatoes and sliced cucumber, if liked.

BONUS POINTS
• Pizza is a great favourite with most children and a good source of protein.
• Boost vitamin and mineral intake by serving pizza with raw vegetables.

OKAY FOR UNDER-ONES?
4–9 months Not suitable. See pages 10–11 and 35–44 for other suggestions.
9–12 months Cut pizza into small strips. Serve, barely warm, as finger food.

EGGY BREAD DOMINOES

Cheap, cheerful and incredibly quick, this is the ideal breakfast, lunch or tea for famished children who can't wait for a meal. It doesn't matter if the bread is slightly stale as it will soon soften once dipped in the egg and milk.
Serves 2–3

3 slices of bread, crusts removed
1 free-range egg
1 tablespoon full-fat milk
2 teaspoons sunflower oil
15 g (½ oz) butter or margarine

To serve:
tomato ketchup
raw carrot and cucumber sticks

Cut each slice of bread into 3 strips. Beat the egg and milk together in a shallow dish. Heat half the oil and butter in a frying pan. Dip one bread strip at a time into the egg mixture, turn with a fork to coat all over, then quickly add to the hot pan. Continue until the pan is full.

Cook for 2–3 minutes each side until golden; remove and keep warm. Heat the rest of the oil and butter in the pan, coat the remaining bread strips in egg and milk, and fry in the same way.

Arrange the eggy bread on serving plates, butting the strips together like dominoes. Add tomato ketchup domino spots and lines, by squirting directly from a plastic ketchup bottle or piping from a greaseproof paper piping bag.

Serve warm, with carrot and cucumber sticks.

BONUS POINT
• Bread plays an important nutritional role in our diet, as part of the grain group. It is a valuable source of carbohydrate, B vitamins, iron and calcium; it also provides protein. Some breads are high in salt; look for reduced-sodium or low-salt bread or – better still – make your own.

OKAY FOR UNDER-ONES?
4–9 months Not suitable. See pages 10–11 and 35–44 for other suggestions.
9–12 months Ideal finger food, but watch your baby closely as the texture is quite soft, enabling a small child to pack quite a lot into his mouth at a time.

• As a variation, shape an eggy bread family, with small gingerbread cutters, adding ketchup features and carrot and cucumber clothes. Or surprise the children with zoo animals or other shapes depending on your selection of cutters.
• For a sweet version, use slices of plain white bread, brioche, panettone or fruit bread. Dip in egg and milk, cook as above, then sprinkle with a little caster sugar and ground cinnamon to serve.

YORKSHIRE PUDDING BASKETS

This recipe is one of my children's firm favourites. To save time you could use ready-made frozen Yorkshire puddings. These are available both pre-cooked and ready-to-bake, though I recommend the latter. **Serves 2–3**

Yorkshire puddings:

a little oil, for brushing

50 g (2 oz) plain flour

1 free-range egg

150 ml (¼ pint) milk and water mixed

Filling:

200 g (7 oz) carrots, diced

75 g (3 oz) fresh or frozen green beans,
   thickly sliced

1 tablespoon sunflower oil

1 tablespoon finely chopped onion

100 g (3½ oz) button mushrooms, sliced

½ garlic clove, crushed

2 teaspoons plain flour

200 ml (7 fl oz) vegetable stock

1 teaspoon low-sodium yeast extract

2 teaspoons tomato ketchup

1 teaspoon chopped fresh rosemary or
   thyme leaves (optional)

• Resist the temptation to open the oven while the Yorkshire puddings are cooking or they may 'sink'.

• Vary the steamed vegetables. Serve frozen peas and mashed parsnips, or broccoli and potato mash if preferred.

Brush 6 sections of a small Yorkshire pudding tin with a little oil and heat in a preheated oven at 200°C (400°F) Gas Mark 6 for 5 minutes while making the batter.

Put the flour into a bowl, add the egg and gradually whisk in the milk and water until smooth and frothy. Pour the batter into the hot tins and bake for 15 minutes until well risen and golden brown.

Meanwhile, put the carrots in a steamer over boiling water and steam for 5 minutes. Add the green beans to the steamer and cook for a further 5 minutes.

While the vegetables are steaming, make the filling. Heat the sunflower oil in a frying pan. Add the onion, mushrooms and garlic and fry, stirring, over a high heat until lightly browned. Sprinkle with the flour and mix well. Stir in the vegetable stock, yeast extract, tomato ketchup and chopped herbs, if using. Allow to simmer for 3–4 minutes.

Loosen the Yorkshire puddings from the tins and transfer to serving plates. Fill them with the mushroom mixture and pile the carrots and beans on top, or serve separately.

BONUS POINT

• A varied range of vegetables ensures a good supply of vitamins and minerals.

OKAY FOR UNDER-ONES?

5–6 months Not suitable. Instead, steam a selection of vegetables and purée with homemade stock or milk until completely smooth.

6–9 months Purée steamed vegetables as above, adding a few plain dried yeast flakes if liked.

9–12 months Suitable provided you use homemade stock for the sauce and a tiny amount of yeast extract. Chop or mash the mushrooms, carrots and green beans to the required texture.

'MISS MOUSE' EGG

This novelty meal is quick and easy to make, and transforms a makeshift tea into something special. **Serves 2**

2 free-range eggs
2 teaspoons ready-made mayonnaise
1 small carrot, coarsely grated
½ red pepper
a little tomato ketchup
15 g (½ oz) medium Cheddar cheese

Put the eggs into a small pan, cover with cold water, bring to the boil and simmer for 8 minutes. Drain, rinse with cold water, then crack the shells and leave in cold water until cool enough to peel.

Cut a lengthways slice from each egg to reveal the yolk. Scoop out the yolk, mix with the mayonnaise and spoon back into the egg white cases. (The slices are not needed.)

Form the grated carrot into nests on 2 serving plates. Put the eggs, stuffed-side down, on top. Add a red pepper slice for each tail, tiny pepper strips for whiskers, and small triangles for ears, positioning these by making tiny slits in the egg white.

Pipe on tomato ketchup eyes and put a cube of cheese in each nest – for the mice to munch on!

OTHER NOVELTY IDEAS
Sailing boats Position the eggs cut-side uppermost on the 'sea' of grated carrot. Cut triangular slices of cheese for sails. Rest these against cocktail stick masts, adding a red pepper or carrot flag to the top of the mast.

Witches toadstools Trim a sliver crossways off the top and bottom of each hard-boiled egg. Stand on plates and top each with an inverted tomato half – to resemble a toadstool. Pipe on mayonnaise or cream cheese dots and sprinkle a little chopped cress around the base of each 'toadstool'.

Humpty Dumpty Trim a sliver crossways off the base of a hard-boiled egg and rest against a wall of sandwiches, cut into strips. Give Humpty trousers and arms shaped from processed cheese slices, positioning these with a little mayonnaise, cream cheese or ketchup. Pipe on ketchup eyes and mouth, and add cress hair.

BONUS POINT
• Eggs are an excellent source of first class protein, vitamin B12 and minerals.

OKAY FOR UNDER-ONES?
Not suitable. See pages 10–12 and 35–55 for other ideas.

• Although young children, pregnant and nursing mothers should avoid homemade mayonnaise as it is made with raw egg yolk, bought mayonnaise isn't a problem because it uses pasteurized eggs but these are usually battery eggs.
• If your children aren't keen on red pepper, use carrot for the features instead.
• Young children may prefer their eggs plain rather than have the yolk mixed with mayonnaise. For very small appetites, halve the hard-boiled eggs and use one egg half for each mouse.

EXTRA SPECIAL PASTA

This smooth veggy pasta sauce is a great way to entice fussy children to eat mixed vegetables without them realising. Vary the vegetables according to what you have in the salad drawer. **Serves 2**

2 teaspoons olive oil
1 small onion, finely chopped
1 small garlic clove, crushed
100 g (3½ oz) carrot, diced
250 g (8 oz) mixed prepared vegetables, such as red pepper, courgette, green beans, celery, mushrooms, butternut squash, diced
200 g (7 oz) can peeled plum tomatoes
large pinch of dried marjoram or oregano
75 g (3 oz) pasta shapes, such as shells or twists
grated Cheddar cheese, to serve

Heat the oil in a pan, add the onion and fry for 4–5 minutes, stirring occasionally, until lightly browned. Add the garlic and vegetables and fry for 2 minutes. Stir in the tomatoes with their juice, and the herbs. Bring to the boil, breaking up the tomatoes with a spoon. Simmer uncovered for 5 minutes, stirring occasionally.

Meanwhile, add the pasta to a pan of boiling water and cook for 8–10 minutes until al dente – tender but firm to the bite.

Purée the tomato mixture in a blender or processor until smooth, then return to the pan. Reheat if necessary.

Drain the pasta, rinse with boiling water and drain again. Add to the sauce, toss well, then spoon into serving bowls. Sprinkle each portion with a little grated cheese.

BONUS POINT
• Children often dislike a particular vegetable because of its texture rather then flavour. Puréeing vegetables and using them in sauces or soups overcomes this problem.

OKAY FOR UNDER-ONES?
4–6 months Not suitable. See pages 10–11 and 35–6 for other suggestions.
6–9 months Mash, finely chop or purée the pasta and sauce together to the required texture.
9–12 months Use a tiny pasta, such as one from the Baby Organics range.

• Flavour the sauce with a few sprigs of fresh herbs from the garden if available – such as basil or marjoram, or a mixture of herbs.

BIG BEAN BURGERS

It can be tricky when non-vegetarian children come to tea, especially if they are confirmed meat eaters. These tasty burgers are a great solution – they look just like standard burgers but are completely meat-free. **Serves 2**

2 teaspoons sunflower oil

1 small onion

1 small garlic clove, crushed

1 teaspoon ground cumin

1 teaspoon ground coriander

½ teaspoon paprika

300 g (10 oz) can black eye beans, drained and rinsed

a little flour

To serve:

2 small soft rolls

few cucumber slices

1 tomato, sliced

a little tomato ketchup or tomato relish

2 slices of cheese (optional)

2 slices of dill cucumber (optional)

Heat half of the oil in a frying pan. Add the onion and garlic and fry, stirring occasionally, for 4–5 minutes until lightly browned. Stir in the spices and cook for 1 minute.

Drain the beans thoroughly, then add to the onion mixture. Mash or briefly process in a blender or food processor. Divide the mixture in half and shape each portion into a burger, using floured hands.

Heat the remaining oil in the clean frying pan and fry the burgers for 3–4 minutes each side until browned.

Split the rolls and arrange cucumber and tomato slices on the bases. Add the burgers and a little ketchup or relish. Top with cheese and dill cucumber if using. Sandwich together with the top halves of the rolls and serve, with a few oven chips if desired.

BONUS POINTS

• Serving beans with bread is an easy way of combining proteins to ensure that all of the essential amino acids can be obtained from one meal.
• Follow this main course with fruit and yogurt for pudding and you have a balanced meal that's much healthier than a shop-bought burger meal.

OKAY FOR UNDER-ONES?

4–9 months Not suitable. See pages 10–11 and 35–44 for other suggestions.
9–12 months Give tiny pieces of burger and strips of bread roll as finger food, along with a little peeled cucumber and pieces of deseeded tomato. Do not serve with ketchup, relish or dill cucumber.

• Buy canned beans without added sugar and salt – usually sold in the organic range of canned foods. Alternatively cook your own beans and freeze in handy sized packs. For this recipe you need 200 g (7 oz) cooked weight.
• Vary the types of beans: chick-peas, or a mixture of red and white kidney beans work well.

CHEESY BLINIS

These mini Russian pancakes are topped with a little butter and served with a colourful salad instead of the traditional smoked salmon and caviar! For speed, I make them with self-raising flour and a little extra baking powder, rather than yeast. **Serves 4**

Blinis:

100 g (3½ oz) self-raising flour

½ teaspoon baking powder

75 g (3 oz) medium Cheddar cheese, grated

1 free-range egg

150 ml (¼ pint) full-fat milk

a little oil, for greasing

Salad:

50 g (2 oz) frozen sweetcorn, just defrosted

2 tomatoes, finely chopped

5 cm (2 inch) piece cucumber, diced

75 g (3 oz) cooked or drained canned red kidney beans

To serve:

a little butter, for spreading

• For a sweet alternative, leave the cheese out of the batter. Serve the blinis topped with yogurt, or butter and jam, or a little chocolate spread for a treat.

• If you have an Aga or Rayburn cooker, you can cook the blinis directly on the simmering plate. (Refer to the manufacturer's instructions.)

First, toss all of the salad ingredients together in a bowl and set aside.

To make the blinis, put the flour, baking powder and cheese into a bowl. Add the egg, then gradually whisk in the milk to make a smooth batter.

Brush a large frying pan or griddle with a little oil and place on a medium heat to heat up.

Cook the blinis in batches. Drop dessertspoonfuls of the batter into the pan (or on to the griddle), spacing them well apart. Cook for 2 minutes until the top is bubbling and the underside is golden. Turn over and cook until the other side is browned.

Wrap the blinis in a clean napkin to keep warm. Cook the rest of them in the same way, brushing the pan with extra oil as needed.

Serve the blinis warm, spread lightly with butter and accompanied by the salad.

BONUS POINTS
• Blinis are a fun 'grain food' alternative to bread.
• Children who aren't keen on cooked vegetables often prefer the crunch and clean taste of raw vegetables in a child-friendly salad.

OKAY FOR UNDER-ONES?
Not suitable, owing to the sodium in self-raising flour and baking powder.

CARROT AND POTATO ROSTI

Most children love this speedy supper as it includes many of their favourite foods. The rösti are quick to prepare, especially if your food processor has a coarse grating disc. Top the rösti with a poached egg if your children are particularly hungry. **Serves 2**

1 medium baking potato, about 250 g (8 oz)

1 carrot, about 125 g (4 oz)

1 slice of onion, finely chopped

1 teaspoon plain flour

1 tablespoon sunflower oil

100 g (3½ oz) broccoli, cut into small florets

200 g (7 oz) can baked beans

Coarsely grate the potato and pat dry with kitchen paper. Coarsely grate the carrot, then mix with the potato, onion and flour.

Heat the oil in a large nonstick frying pan and drop dessertspoonfuls of the potato mixture into the pan, spreading the vegetables into a thin even layer. Cook for 3–4 minutes each side until golden, and the potato is cooked.

Meanwhile, steam the broccoli over boiling water for 5 minutes. Warm the baked beans in a bowl in the microwave, or in a small pan on the hob.

Drain the rösti well on kitchen paper and arrange on plates with the broccoli and baked beans to serve.

BONUS POINT

• Although the vitamin C content of potatoes is low, its contribution is valuable because most of us eat a relatively large amount of this staple food. This applies especially to children who are reluctant fruit eaters.

OKAY FOR UNDER-ONES?

5–6 months Not suitable. Instead, cook the potato, carrot and broccoli in formula milk or water and purée until smooth.

6–9 months Cook the vegetables as above and purée to the desired texture with a little milk if needed.

9–12 months Cook the potato and carrot in a little boiling water and steam some broccoli above. Mash the vegetables with baked beans.

• Vary the rösti mixture if you like – try a mixture of grated potato, carrot and courgette; or grated sweet potato and ordinary potato; or simply use all potato.

• If preferred, the rösti can be baked in the oven. Place on an oiled baking sheet, brush the tops with a little oil and bake at 200°C (400°F) Gas Mark 6 for 15 minutes.

OPEN SANDWICH

Make an ordinary sandwich more appealing by presenting it as one of your child's favourite toys. With a little imagination you could make a cruise ship, rocket, car or doll's pram – as easily as this train. **Serves 2**

2 slices of bread

butter or margarine, for spreading

a little yeast extract (optional)

2 thin slices of Cheddar cheese

¼ cucumber

1 carrot, cut into long thin slices

1 cherry tomato, halved

a little salad cress

Cut each slice of bread roughly into a train shape, remembering to include the driver's cab. Spread lightly with butter or margarine and yeast extract, if using, then cover each 'engine' with a slice of cheese, trimming to fit. Place each train on a serving plate.

Cut 6 slices of cucumber for the wheels and position on the trains. Shape 2 funnels and 2 driver's cabs from carrot slices and apply these. Cut 2 wedges of cucumber for the cab roofs; position these and put a halved tomato on each engine. To finish, apply carrot strips to the engines and add a trail of snipped cress for 'smoke'.

BONUS POINTS
• Novelty sandwiches are a good way to encourage your child's interest in food. Get them to think up ideas for different sandwiches.
• Mini sandwiches make healthy, energy packed snacks to boost energy levels during the day.

OKAY FOR UNDER-ONES?
4–9 months Not suitable. See pages 10–11 and 35–44 for other suggestions.
9–12 months Offer small cubes of cheese, strips of bread and butter, sticks of peeled cucumber and a little carrot to eat as finger foods.

• If your children don't like cress, use a little tomato ketchup squirted from a plastic ketchup bottle or piped from a greaseproof paper piping bag instead.
• For children on a vegan or dairy-free diet, spread bread with hummus, or peanut butter provided allergy isn't a consideration.

Let's get fruity

These fresh and fruity puds are great treats for those occasions when the family can sit down and enjoy a meal together – or for your children to share with visiting friends. These recipes are lower in sugar and fat than most alternative puddings.

DREAMY DUNKERS

This is a great recipe to tempt those children who are reluctant to eat fruit. You can make the sauce in advance, but the fruits are best prepared at the last minute. **Serves 4**

Chocolate sauce:

50 g (2 oz) good quality milk chocolate

75 g (3 oz) good quality plain chocolate

75 ml (3 fl oz) full-fat milk

2 teaspoons golden syrup

Dunkers:

1 red-skinned apple, cored

2 peaches, stoned

1 kiwi fruit, peeled

250 g (9 oz) strawberries

1 banana, peeled

Break the chocolate into pieces and put into a small pan with the milk and golden syrup. Heat gently, stirring occasionally, until melted and smooth. Pour the chocolate sauce into 4 small dishes and set each one on a larger individual serving plate.

Cut the apple, peaches and kiwi fruit into chunks. Halve or quarter the strawberries, depending on size. Thickly slice the banana.

Arrange the fruit on the serving plates. Provide small forks to enable children to dunk the fruits into the warm sauce before eating.

VARIATION

Strawberry fondue Purée 100 g (3½ oz) strawberries, sieve to remove seeds, then stir into 200 g (7 oz) Greek yogurt. Sweeten with 1–2 teaspoons caster sugar if required. Spoon into small dishes and serve with fruits for dipping, as above.

OKAY FOR UNDER-ONES?

4–6 months Not suitable. Instead, serve a little cooked, puréed and sieved apple – mixed into a little baby rice if preferred.

6–9 months Purée or mash some peach with a few strawberries, then press through a sieve. Stir in a little cooked apple purée, or some natural bio yogurt. As strawberries can cause an allergic reaction in young children, you should offer tiny first tastes.

9–12 months Serve the fruit without the chocolate sauce – as finger food. Cut the apple and peach into slices rather than chunks, so they will be easier for your baby to manage.

• For a cheat's chocolate sauce to serve one child, melt 2 tablespoons chocolate spread with 1 tablespoon full-fat milk in the microwave; stir until smooth.

• Children also love chocolate sauce served with fruit-filled pancakes, or with sliced bananas and vanilla ice cream.

PINK BLUSH JELLIES

Most children love jellies, but packets of flavoured jelly invariably include animal products, not to mention artificial flavourings and a high level of sugar. These individual fruit jellies are made with redcurrant juice, strawberries and grapes, and set with Vege-Gel for a vitamin C-packed, low-sugar dessert. **Serves 4**

125 g (4 oz) redcurrants, stalks removed
250 ml (8 fl oz) water
100 g (3½ oz) strawberries
75 g (3 oz) seedless red grapes, halved
300 ml (½ pint) apple juice
1 sachet Vege-Gel
50 g (2 oz) caster sugar
redcurrant sprigs, to decorate (optional)

Rinse the redcurrants and put into a saucepan with the water. Bring to the boil and simmer for 5 minutes. Press through a sieve to remove skins.

Divide the strawberries and grapes between four 150 ml (¼ pint) individual jelly moulds.

Pour the apple juice into a saucepan, sprinkle in the Vege-Gel and stir until dissolved, then add the redcurrant juice and sugar. Bring to the boil, stirring, until thickened, then pour straight into the jelly moulds. Allow to cool, then refrigerate for 2–3 hours until set.

To turn each jelly out, briefly dip the mould into a bowl of very hot water. Loosen the edges with your fingertips and invert the mould on to a serving plate. Holding the mould and plate together, jerk the mould to release the jelly, then remove.

Serve the jellies topped with redcurrant sprigs if liked.

BONUS POINT
• Redcurrants are a good source of vitamin C; they also contain useful amounts of potassium.

OKAY FOR UNDER-ONES?
Not suitable. See pages 10–12 and 35–55 for other ideas.

• If preferred, 1 sliced small banana can be used in place of the strawberries.
• During the winter months, use frozen mixed soft fruits in place of the redcurrants and strawberries.
• Make sure the hot jelly mixture comes to the boil or it will not set in the fridge.
• For children who hate bits, purée the fruits and stir into the jelly.

RAINBOW SUNDAES

For this delicious alternative to bought fruit yogurt, a creamy pudding – made from quick-cooking millet flakes – is mixed with natural bio yogurt and layered with an assortment of fruits. **Serves 4**

25 g (1 oz) millet flakes

300 ml (½ pint) full-fat milk

2 kiwi fruit, peeled

2 ripe peaches or nectarines, halved
   and stoned

150 g (5 oz) strawberries

150 g (5 oz) natural bio yogurt

2–3 tablespoons caster sugar (optional)

Put the millet flakes and milk into a small pan and slowly bring to the boil. Simmer gently, stirring constantly, for 3–4 minutes, until thickened and creamy, rather like the consistency of porridge. Take off the heat, cover and leave to cool. Meanwhile finely chop the fruits, keeping them separate.

Fold the yogurt and sugar, if using, into the cooled millet mixture. Spoon the chopped kiwi fruit into the base of four 250 ml (8 fl oz) small plastic or glass serving dishes. Cover with half of the yogurt mixture, then the chopped peaches. Spoon the remaining yogurt mixture over the peaches and top with the strawberries.

Chill the sundaes in the refrigerator until ready to serve.

BONUS POINTS

• The fruits in this pudding provide plenty of vitamin C – essential for keeping bones, teeth and skin healthy, to aid healing and to assist the absorption of calcium and iron. Here vitamin C enables the body to absorb more of the calcium in the yogurt.

• Available from healthfood shops as whole grains or quick cooking flakes, millet is gluten free and a good source of protein.

OKAY FOR UNDER-ONES?

Do not add sugar.

5–6 months Cook half the quantity of millet flakes with formula milk, or water. Cool, then flavour with a little finely mashed banana or puréed cooked apple or pear.

6–9 months Purée and sieve 1 ripe peach. Stir into a little cooled millet and yogurt mixture.

9–12 months Serve a half portion of the sundae (without added sugar). Or flavour the millet and yogurt mixture with one of the fruits, puréed and sieved.

• As a variation, purée and sieve the fruits before layering with the millet mixture.

• Use just one type of fruit for a simple dessert.

• As an alternative to millet, layer the fruits with rice pudding mixed with a little yogurt, or just plain yogurt if preferred.

DATE & ORANGE FOOL

Even the flavour of mild creamy bio yogurt can be a little too much for young children. Mix it with naturally sweet date purée and you are sure to win them round. **Serves 4**

2 large oranges, freshly squeezed
125 g (4 oz) stoned dates
300 g (10 oz) natural bio yogurt
1 banana, sliced, to serve

Make the orange juice up to 275 ml (9 fl oz) with water and put into a small pan with the dates. Bring to the boil, cover and simmer for 10 minutes until soft. Allow to cool slightly, then purée in a food processor or blender until smooth. Set aside until completely cooled.

Put alternate spoonfuls of date purée and yogurt in 4 small serving dishes, then swirl together attractively, using a small knife or skewer. Chill in the refrigerator until required.

Top the fruit fools with sliced banana just before serving.

BONUS POINTS

• Dates are a rich source of potassium and contain smaller amounts of iron, magnesium and niacin.
• Dates also have a mild gentle laxative effect. If your child is a little constipated, offer a few stoned dates to munch on – these should do the trick without irritating the bowel or stomach.

OKAY FOR UNDER-ONES?

4–6 months Not suitable. Instead, give some very finely mashed banana.
6–9 months Offer a little well mashed banana folded into some yogurt.
9–12 months Give your baby the yogurt combined with a tiny taster of the date and orange purée at first (to ensure there is no adverse reaction).

• Prunes, figs or dried apricots may be used instead of dates.
• As a variation, the date purée and yogurt can be layered in small plastic or glass dishes.
• Encourage your children to brush their teeth after a meal, especially after a dessert. Although there is no added sugar here, the natural sugar in the dates and the acid in the oranges can cause problems for tooth enamel.
• Date and orange purée also makes a great spread for toast, or a filling for a simple Victoria sandwich, and it is much lower in sugar than jam. Make as above, but only add enough water to make up to 250 ml (8 fl oz). Store in a sealed plastic container or jar in the fridge up to 1 week.

MINI BANANA CASTLES

These mini sponge puddings with their vibrant raspberry sauce are the perfect ending to a special family meal. For a decorative effect, spoon dots of Greek yogurt around the edge of the sauce and feather into teardrops using a skewer. **Serves 4**

50 g (2 oz) soft margarine

50 g (2 oz) self-raising flour

25 g (1 oz) caster sugar

25 g (1 oz) ground almonds

½ teaspoon baking powder

1 free-range egg

1 small ripe banana, about 125 g (4 oz) unpeeled weight

Raspberry sauce:

250 g (8 oz) frozen raspberries

4 teaspoons icing sugar

Lightly oil four 150 ml (¼ pint) individual metal pudding moulds and line the bases with rounds of greaseproof paper.

Put the margarine, flour, sugar, ground almonds and baking powder into a bowl or food processor. Add the egg and beat until smooth. Mash the banana and stir into the mixture. Divide between the prepared moulds and level the surface.

Bake in a preheated oven at 180°C (350°F) Gas Mark 4 for 15 minutes until well risen and golden, and the tops spring back when lightly pressed with a fingertip.

Meanwhile, make the raspberry sauce. Set aside 75 g (3 oz) of the raspberries. Purée the rest of them and sieve to remove the seeds, then mix with 3 teaspoons of the icing sugar. Spoon on to 4 serving plates.

Loosen the puddings from their moulds with a round-bladed knife, then turn out and peel off the lining paper. Stand a pudding on each plate – on a pool of sauce. Arrange the reserved raspberries on the sponges and sift the remaining icing sugar over the top to decorate.

BONUS POINTS

• Bananas are an easily digested energy food. They are rich in potassium, which helps to regulate blood pressure and aids muscle and nerve function. As bananas are naturally very sweet when ripe, they reduce the amount of sugar needed here.

• Raspberries are rich in vitamin C, which is needed for healthy skin, bones and teeth, plus healing and the absorption of iron. They also contain some vitamin E, folate and fibre.

OKAY FOR UNDER-ONES?

Not suitable.

5–6 months Instead, offer a little well mashed banana.

6–12 months Offer a little mashed banana mixed with some puréed and unsweetened sieved raspberry purée. Or mix banana with some natural bio yogurt, chopping the fruit or mashing it coarsely for older babies.

• Strawberries can be used instead of raspberries.

• If fresh berries are out of season, use frozen ones or some frozen mixed berry fruits instead.

• Small metal pudding moulds are available from good cook shops and will last a lifetime. Or you can use thick demi-tasse coffee cups instead.

• These puddings can be made ahead, turned out and reheated individually in the microwave for 20 seconds on High.

APPLE STRUDEL ROLL-UPS

These tiny individual strudels – made with filo pastry and naturally sweet dessert apples – are just the right size for tiny hands to hold. **Makes 12**

2 dessert apples

50 g (2 oz) sultanas

1 tablespoon caster sugar

large pinch of ground cinnamon

3 sheets filo pastry (from a 275 g (9 oz) chilled pack)

40 g (1½ oz) butter, melted

icing sugar, for dusting

Peel, quarter, core and finely chop the apples. Place in a bowl with the sultanas, sugar and cinnamon; mix together.

Lay one of the pastry sheets on a clean surface with one of the longest edges towards you; keep the rest covered with a damp cloth to prevent them drying out. Cut the filo sheet into 4 strips, each about 25 cm (10 inch) long. Brush the strips lightly with butter. Divide one-third of the filling between them, spooning it on to the ends closest to you.

One strip at a time, fold in the long edges of the pastry towards the filling, then roll up like a parcel to enclose the filling. Place join-side down on a lightly oiled baking sheet.

Do the same with the other strips, then repeat with the remaining two pastry sheets, to make 12 filo rolls in total.

Brush with the remaining melted butter and bake in a preheated oven at 180°C (350°F) Gas Mark 4 for 10–12 minutes until golden. Dust lightly with sifted icing sugar and serve warm or cold.

BONUS POINTS

• Apples provide vitamin C, which is an antioxidant and helps protect the body from infections.
• Children need fat such as butter, in moderation, for the concentrated energy and fat-soluble vitamins that it provides.

OKAY FOR UNDER-ONES?

5–6 months Not suitable. Instead, serve smooth cooked apple purée on its own or mixed with a little baby rice and formula milk or water. Choose sweet dessert apples such as Gala, rather than tart varieties like Granny Smith.
6–12 months Serve puréed cooked dessert apple mixed with a little yogurt or fromage frais.
9–12 months Serve these little pastries as an occasional finger food treat, or cut into tiny pieces. Alternatively, serve a little cooked, mashed apple on its own or with yogurt or fromage frais.

• Filo pastry tends to dry out rapidly, so wrap any that you don't need for the strudels immediately and freeze for another occasion.
• As a variation, make apple purses. Cut one pastry sheet into 8 squares. Brush 4 squares with butter, then top each with another square, at an angle to form an 8-pointed star. Spoon the filing into the centre. Bring the pastry corners up over the filling and pinch together to seal. Repeat with the other 2 pastry sheets.

WARM PLUM TRIFLE

This tempting pud with its creamy custard base, ruby fruit layer and light fluffy marshmallow meringue topping is equally popular with children and grown-ups. It's the ideal pudding to impress Granny! Select ripe plums for their natural sweetness. **Serves 4**

3 free-range eggs, separated
125 g (4 oz) caster sugar
grated rind of 1 orange
75 g (3 oz) breadcrumbs
450 ml (¾ pint) full-fat milk
400 g (13 oz) plums, stoned and sliced
3 tablespoons plum or strawberry jam

• As an alternative to plums, use fresh strawberries, bottled stoned cherries, or frozen mixed summer fruits. There's no need to cook these fruits: simply slice strawberries; drain cherries well; defrost and drain frozen fruits thoroughly.
• The custard may be cooked in advance but the meringue is best applied just before baking.

Butter a 1.2 litre (2 pint) ovenproof pie or soufflé dish. Put the egg yolks in a bowl with 2 tablespoons of the sugar and the orange rind. Mix well, then stir in the breadcrumbs.

Put the milk in a small pan, bring just to the boil, then whisk into the egg yolk mixture. Pour into the prepared dish and bake in a preheated oven at 180°C (350°F) Gas Mark 4 for 20–25 minutes until set and just browning around the edges.

Meanwhile, put the plums into a shallow pan with 2 tablespoons water. Cover and poach for 5 minutes or until just tender. Drain thoroughly.

Take the baked custard out of the oven and reduce the setting to 150°C (300°F) Gas Mark 2. Dot the jam over the top of the custard and top with the poached plums.

Whisk the egg whites in a bowl until stiffly peaking, but not dry. Gradually whisk in the remaining sugar, a teaspoonful at a time, and continue whisking until the meringue is thick and glossy.

Spoon the meringue over the plums, swirling it attractively with the back of a spoon. Bake for 20–25 minutes until the meringue is pale golden and well cooked. Serve warm.

BONUS POINTS
• Plums contain vitamin E, an antioxidant that helps to protect cells, and may help to retard the effects of ageing. They are also a good source of potassium, which is needed to regulate heartbeat and blood pressure.
• Eggs yolks are a good source of iron – needed for healthy blood cells – and chromium, which helps to control fat levels and cholesterol in the blood. Eggs are also a valuable source of zinc for vegetarians.

OKAY FOR UNDER-ONES?
Sweetened puddings, such as this, should not be given to children under one.
5–6 months Offer a little cooked plum purée, or mixed plum and pear purée.
6–12 months As above. Serve fruit purée plain or mixed into a little yogurt or fromage frais (see left). Adjust the consistency of the purée to suit your baby.

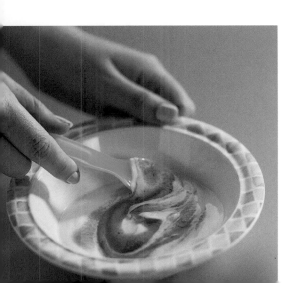

LACY APRICOT PANCAKES

All children – big and small – love pancakes. Here the batter is drizzled into the pan from a spoon to create a lacy effect, and the resulting light pancakes are filled with an apricot and apple compote. **Serves 4**

Pancakes:

50 g (2 oz) plain flour

1 free-range egg

125 ml (4 fl oz) full-fat milk

1 teaspoon sunflower oil, plus extra for frying

Filling:

375 g (12 oz) fresh apricots, stoned and diced

1 dessert apple, quartered, cored, peeled and diced

4 tablespoons apple juice

4 scoops vanilla ice cream

To finish:

sifted icing sugar, to decorate

• Use dried or canned apricots when fresh ones are out of season, or substitute ripe plums.
• If time is short, rather than make a compote, serve pancakes with a little pear and apricot spread. Available from healthfood shops, this is additive and sugar free. Don't be put off by the unappetising dark colour – it tastes delicious.

For the filling, put the apricots, apple and apple juice into a small saucepan, cover and simmer for 5 minutes. Set aside to cool slightly.

To make the pancakes, put the flour into a bowl, add the egg and gradually whisk in the milk until smooth and frothy. Whisk in 1 teaspoon oil.

Heat a little oil in a small frying pan until it is very hot; pour off any excess oil. Drizzle pancake batter over the base of the pan to give a lacy effect. Cook for 2–3 minutes until golden, then loosen the pancake, toss and cook until the other side is golden.

Slide the pancake on to a warm plate and keep hot. Continue making pancakes in this way until all the batter is used, stacking the cooked pancakes interleaved with greaseproof paper.

To serve, put a pancake on each serving plate and place a spoonful of the warm apricot compote and a scoop of ice cream on one side. Fold the pancake over the filling and dust lightly with icing sugar.

BONUS POINT

• Fresh apricots are a good source of beta-carotene, the plant form of vitamin A; they contain twice as much as canned apricots.

OKAY FOR UNDER-ONES?

5–6 months Not suitable. Instead, cook apricots and apples in a little water. Purée, then press through a sieve to remove apricot skins.
6–9 months Purée cooked apricots and apples, then sieve to remove skins. Serve on its own or mixed with a little natural bio yogurt or fromage frais.
9–12 months Serve mashed cooked fruits with a little ice cream. Give your baby some strips of pancake to pick up and eat.

LOVELY LOLLIES

All children love lollies and they're a fun way to encourage children to eat more dairy foods and try new fruits. **Makes 8**

1 litre (1¾ pints) full-fat milk
1 tablespoon caster sugar
few drops of vanilla essence (optional)

Pour the milk into a large heavy-based saucepan and bring to the boil. Reduce the heat and simmer uncovered, stirring occasionally, for 1½ hours or until the milk has reduced by just over half – to about 400 ml (14 fl oz).

Stir in the sugar, cool, then strain into two 4-section lolly moulds. Add the plastic handle tops and freeze until solid.

To serve, dip the lolly moulds into hot water for a count of 10, then flex the handles and remove the lollies from their moulds.

VARIATIONS

Strawberry crush Purée 150 g (5 oz) strawberries in a blender or food processor, then press through a sieve to remove the seeds. Mix with two 40 g (1½ oz) mini pots of strawberry fromage frais. Pour into a 4-section lolly mould. Freeze and unmould as above. **Makes 4**

Spotty orange lollies Pour 200 ml (7 fl oz) orange juice (from a carton) into a 4-section lolly mould and freeze until mushy. Drop 1 small pack Jelly Tots into the semi-frozen mixture. Freeze and unmould as above. **Makes 4**

Busy bees Put 125 g (4 oz) blackberries or blackcurrants into a small pan with 1 tablespoon caster sugar and 1 tablespoon water. Cover and cook for 5 minutes until just soft. Purée until smooth, then sieve and leave to cool. Purée 2 stoned ripe peaches or nectarines until smooth, then sieve. Spoon 1 teaspoon peach or nectarine purée into the base of 4 lolly moulds. Freeze until solid, then spoon 1 teaspoon of blackberry or blackcurrant purée on top. Freeze again until solid. Repeat until the moulds are full. Freeze and unmould as above. **Makes 4**

BONUS POINT
• Make your own lollies and you can rest assured that they are free from artificial colourings, flavourings and sweeteners.

OKAY FOR UNDER-ONES?
Not suitable.

• Lolly moulds vary considerably in size, the ones illustrated each hold 60 ml (2 fl oz) per section. You may need to double up the recipes if your moulds are significantly larger.
• Experiment with different fruit purées.
• Lollies can be very soothing for teething toddlers.

FRUIT SMOOTHIES

Some toddlers go off drinking milk once they stop using a bottle. These fruit-enriched drinks – based on milk, yogurt or soft cheese – are tempting and highly nutritious. Serve as a healthy snack, breakfast treat or dessert.
Each serves 2

100 g (3½ oz) raspberries, defrosted if
    frozen
2 ripe peaches, halved, stoned and
    roughly chopped
4 tablespoons fromage frais
200 ml (7 fl oz) full-fat milk

Put the raspberries, peaches, fromage frais and milk into a blender or food processor and work until smooth. Pass through a sieve, then pour into glasses. Serve with straws.

VARIATIONS
Strawberry crush Purée and sieve 100 g (3½ oz) strawberries. Whisk with 200 g (7 oz) Greek yogurt and 200 ml (7 fl oz) full-fat milk. Sweeten with a little caster sugar if required. Pour into tall glasses and top with strawberry slices.

Apricot smoothie Tip a 411 g (13½ oz) can apricot halves in natural juice into a blender or food processor. Add 100 g (3½ oz) ricotta cheese and process until smooth. Pour into glasses and serve with straws.

Banana and chocolate duet Put 2 thickly sliced small bananas, 2 scoops chocolate ice cream and 300 ml (½ pint) full-fat milk into a blender or food processor and blend until smooth and frothy. Pour into glasses and top with a sprinkling of grated chocolate or drinking chocolate powder.

BONUS POINTS
• These dairy-rich drinks are packed with calcium, vitamin A and vitamin D – and boosted with vitamin C from the fresh fruit.
• Vitamin C, obtained from fruit, is essential for healthy skin, teeth and bones; it also aids the absorption of calcium from the dairy products in these drinks.

OKAY FOR UNDER-ONES?
Do not give smoothies that contain ice cream or sugar to under-ones.
5–6 months Not suitable. Instead, offer a little sieved peach purée stirred into a little baby rice.
6–9 months Reduce the amount of milk and serve as a pudding rather than a drink.
9–12 months Dilute drinks with extra milk so that they will go through the holes in a feeder beaker, or offer from an open cup.

• Experiment with your own combinations of fruit and milk, yogurt or soft cheese.
• Encourage young children to help make smoothies – measuring the ingredients, or perhaps dressing up glasses with curly straws or stirrers.

Lunchbox specials

As you won't be overseeing your children's lunch at school or nursery it's reassuring to know that you've sent them off with a healthy and satisfying meal. Include a mini frozen ice pack to keep the lunch cool. Also make sure the lunchbox is named and easily identifiable by a picture sticker – especially important for small children who haven't yet learnt to read.

MINI PASTA SALAD

If your child refuses to eat salad – especially one that features green vegetables – this chunky pasta salad might be just the recipe to convert him. Make it the night before and store in the fridge. When you have pasta for supper, cook a little extra and use 125 g (4 oz) of the cooked pasta to make the salad. **Serves 2**

50 g (2 oz) small pasta shapes

2 tablespoons sunflower oil

1 teaspoon sun-dried or ordinary tomato paste, or ketchup

1 teaspoon wine vinegar

½ small carrot, diced

¼ red pepper, deseeded and diced

1 tomato, diced

50 g (2 oz) medium Cheddar cheese, diced

Add the pasta to a saucepan of boiling water and cook until al dente – just tender.

Meanwhile mix the sunflower oil, tomato paste or ketchup and vinegar in a bowl until evenly blended. Add the diced carrot, red pepper, tomato and cheese; toss to mix.

Drain the pasta, rinse under cold running water and drain thoroughly. Add the pasta to the salad, toss together and divide between 2 small plastic containers. Seal well and pack into lunchboxes, or refrigerate if making the salad the night before.

BONUS POINTS

• Tomatoes, carrots and red peppers are all rich in beta-carotene – the bright yellow-orange pigment that is converted by the body into vitamin A. The more intense the colour of the vegetable or fruit, the more beta-carotene it contains. Beta-carotene is also important as an antioxidant and may help reduce the risk of some cancers.

OKAY FOR UNDER-ONES?
4–9 months Not suitable.
9–12 months Make the salad without the dressing. Offer as finger food.

WHAT ELSE TO PACK?
• easy-peel satsuma, kiwi fruit wedges, or strawberries
• date muffin (see page 117)
• water, or blackcurrant juice diluted with water to drink

BIG BEAN BONANZA

Make this easy salad the night before to save that early morning panic. If you are only preparing one child's packed lunch, save the other portion for your lunch – pile it on to salad leaves and top with garlicky roasted peppers.
Serves 2

40 g (1½ oz) bulgar wheat

25 g (1 oz) frozen broad beans

25 g (1 oz) green beans, thickly sliced

2 tablespoons frozen peas

1 orange

1 tomato, chopped

40 g (1½ oz) canned red kidney beans, drained

2 teaspoons olive oil

Put the bulgar wheat into a bowl, pour on 150 ml (¼ pint) boiling water and leave to soak for 10 minutes. Meanwhile, cook the broad beans, green beans and peas in a small saucepan of boiling water for 3 minutes. Drain, rinse with cold water and drain again.

Halve the orange lengthwise and cut out the segments from one half; squeeze the juice from the other half.

Drain off any excess water from the bulgar wheat, then add the cooked vegetables, tomato, red kidney beans, orange segments, 1 tablespoon orange juice and the oil. Toss to mix and divide between 2 small plastic containers. Seal well.

BONUS POINT
• Combining pulses such as red kidney beans with cereals such as wheat, rice, pasta or bread provides all the essential amino acids required to make up complete protein in one meal.

OKAY FOR UNDER-ONES?
4–9 months Not suitable.
9–12 months When your baby readily accepts texture, finely chop a small portion of the vegetables and mix into soaked couscous with a little oil and orange juice.

WHAT ELSE TO PACK?
• mini fromage frais, plastic spoon
• a small soft roll
• box of mini raisins
• water, or apple juice diluted with water to drink

• If your children aren't keen on the nutty flavour of bulgar wheat, use soaked couscous, or cooked rice or pasta instead.
• Vary the vegetables as you like – broccoli, sweetcorn and frozen mixed veggies are suitable options.

TAKEAWAY TORTILLA

Cook an extra potato when you have supper and use it to make this easy Spanish-style omelette the following morning, while your child is busy eating breakfast. You can always add a few frozen veggies in place of fresh ones for convenience. If preferred, pop the tortilla halves into a halved pitta bread with a few slices of tomato or a little ketchup. **Serves 1**

1 teaspoon sunflower oil

50 g (2 oz) cooked potato, diced

2.5 cm (1 inch) piece courgette, diced

1 button mushroom, sliced

1 slice of onion, finely chopped

½ garlic clove, crushed (optional)

1 free-range egg

salt and black pepper (optional)

Heat the oil in a small 11 cm (4½ inch) nonstick frying pan (see below) and add the vegetables and garlic, if using. Fry, stirring, for 4–5 minutes until the potatoes are lightly browned.

Beat the egg in a bowl with a little seasoning if required, then pour over the vegetables in the pan. Fry over a medium heat until the underside is browned. Place the pan under a medium grill for a few minutes until the egg on the surface is cooked and golden.

Allow the tortilla to cool, then cut in half and wrap in foil.

BONUS POINT
• Quick and easy to make, this high protein, high energy lunch will keep your child sustained until it's time to come home.

OKAY FOR UNDER-ONES?
4–9 months Not suitable.
9–12 months Make sure the omelette is well cooked. Cut into pieces so that your baby can pick it up to eat, or finely chop and serve from a spoon, adding a little milk if required. Offer a few strips of pitta as well, if wished.

WHAT ELSE TO PACK?

• sliced brown bread sandwiched together with a little sunflower and raisin butter. Make in advance and freeze – pop into the lunchbox still frozen; it will defrost by lunchtime.

• carrot and cucumber sticks in a foil package

• halved kiwi fruit (to eat boiled-egg style), plus teaspoon

• water, or orange juice diluted half and half with water to drink

---

• Look out for a mini frying pan in a good cookshop, or hypermarket if you are on holiday in France. My son loves the novelty of having a pan especially for him. Alternatively use an ordinary small pan: scoop the fried vegetables into the middle, surround with a large biscuit cutter and pour in the beaten egg. Make sure the pan is suitable for placing under the grill.

PICNIC PIES

These are made in sections of a muffin tin to ensure that they are just the right size for a young child to hold; there is sufficient depth for plenty of the tasty quiche-style filling. Make the day before and refrigerate until required. If you are short of time, use a 375 g (12 oz) pack frozen shortcrust pastry.
Makes 12

Pastry:

100 g (3½ oz) plain flour

100 g (3½ oz) wholemeal flour

50 g (2 oz) block margarine, diced

50 g (2 oz) white vegetable shortening, diced

3–4 tablespoons water

Filling:

100 g (3½ oz) medium Cheddar cheese, grated

2 tomatoes, thinly sliced

3 free-range eggs

300 ml (½ pint) full-fat milk

salt and black pepper

Lightly oil 12 sections of a muffin tin. To make the pastry, put the flours into a bowl, add the fats and rub into the flour using your fingertips (or an electric mixer) until the mixture resembles fine breadcrumbs. Add enough water to mix to a smooth dough.

Lightly knead the dough and roll out thinly on a lightly floured surface. Stamp out 10 cm (4 inch) rounds, using a fluted cutter (or an upturned individual flan tin or small saucer as a guide). Use to line the muffin tin, gently pressing the pastry into the edges. Re-roll pastry trimmings and cut more rounds as needed.

Divide two-thirds of the cheese between the pastry cases. Add the sliced tomatoes, halving them to fit if large.

Beat the eggs and milk together in a bowl with a little seasoning. Pour into the tart cases and sprinkle with the remaining cheese. Bake in a preheated oven at 180°C (350°F) Gas Mark 4 for 20–25 minutes until golden and the filling is set.

Loosen the pastry edges with a small knife and leave the pies to cool in the tin. Transfer to a plastic box and store in the fridge for up to 2 days.

FLAVOUR VARIATIONS
• Add ½ cored, deseeded and finely chopped red pepper, and 75 g (3 oz) canned or defrosted frozen sweetcorn.
• Add 100 g (3½ oz) sliced button mushrooms.
• Add 75 g (3 oz) frozen spinach, defrosted and well drained.

BONUS POINT
• Combining brown and white flours is a good way of introducing children to wholemeal flour.

OKAY FOR UNDER-ONES?
4–9 months Not suitable.
9–12 months Cut tarts into quarters and serve as finger food.

WHAT ELSE TO PACK?
• small plastic box of cucumber sticks, cherry tomatoes and seedless grapes
• mini fromage frais, plastic spoon
• slice of malt loaf
• water, or apple juice diluted with water to drink

MUFFIN MANIA

These deliciously moist banana and chocolate chip muffins are made with naturally sweet fruit so there's no need to add extra sugar. **Makes 12**

200 g (7 oz) self-raising flour

½ teaspoon baking powder

2 free-range eggs, beaten

5 tablespoons sunflower oil

5 tablespoons full-fat milk

1 teaspoon vanilla essence

2 ripe bananas, about 325 g (11 oz)
    unpeeled weight

100 g (3½ oz) milk chocolate dots

Line a 12-hole muffin tray with paper muffin cases. Sift the flour and baking powder together into a mixing bowl. Beat the eggs, oil, milk and vanilla essence together in a separate bowl.

Mash the bananas on a plate, using a fork, then add to the flour with the egg mixture and fork the ingredients together briefly until only just mixed. Stir in the chocolate dots.

Spoon into the paper cases and bake in a preheated oven at 200°C (400°F) Gas Mark 6 for 15 minutes until the muffins are well risen and the tops spring back when lightly pressed with the fingertips.

Transfer to a wire rack to cool. Store in an airtight tin for up to 2 days.

VARIATION

Date muffins Increase the baking powder to 1 teaspoon. Put 175 g (6 oz) stoned and chopped dates into a saucepan and add 300 ml (½ pint) water. Bring to the boil, then simmer for 5 minutes. Let cool slightly, then purée in a blender until smooth, or break up the dates with a wooden spoon. Mix with the other ingredients and bake as above.

BONUS POINT

• A subtle way to encourage reluctant fruit eaters.

OKAY FOR UNDER-ONES?

Not suitable, as self-raising flour and baking powder contain sodium.

WHAT ELSE TO PACK?

• hummus and cucumber sandwiches

• few cherry tomatoes and a few seedless grapes

• mini fromage frais, plastic spoon

• water, or orange juice diluted half and half with water to drink

---

• These muffins are good freezer standbys. When cool, pack in a plastic container, seal and freeze for up to 6 weeks. You can add a frozen muffin to a lunchbox – it will be defrosted by lunchtime.

• For tiny appetites bake the mixture in petit four cases set in a mini muffin tin for 8–10 minutes; for small muffins bake in standard paper cake cases in a bun tray, allowing 10–12 minutes.

Bake together

Cooking with children can be fun and a great way to teach them different skills. Weighing out ingredients gives them familiarity with numbers, while mixing, spreading and spooning aid co-ordination. Even the fussiest of eaters can become the most enthusiastic of cooks! So pull up a sturdy chair, keep a close eye, and don't worry about the mess ...

NOUGHTS & CROSSES

These cheesy biscuits seem to melt in the mouth. Get your small helper to weigh out the ingredients, roll the dough and help with shaping. **Makes 20**

75 g (3 oz) wholemeal flour (or white, or half wholemeal/half white flour)

75 g (3 oz) butter or block margarine, diced

75 g (3 oz) medium Cheddar cheese, grated

1 free-range egg, separated

1 tablespoon sesame seeds (optional)

Put the flour into a bowl, add the butter and rub in using your fingertips (or a mixer) until the mixture resembles fine breadcrumbs. Stir in the cheese, then mix in the egg yolk to make a smooth dough.

Gently knead the dough, then roll out on a lightly floured surface to a 5 mm (¼ inch) thickness. Cut out rounds, using a 6 cm (2½ inch) plain round cutter. From these, cut noughts, using a 3 cm (1¼ inch) plain round cutter. Using a palette knife, carefully lift the noughts on to a large baking sheet.

Draw a broad cross on a piece of card, about 6 cm (2½ inches) high. Cut out and use as a template to cut crosses from the dough. Lift the crosses on to the baking sheet. Re-roll trimmings to cut more shapes.

Brush with egg white and sprinkle with sesame seeds, if using. Bake in a preheated oven at 190°C (375°F) Gas Mark 5 for 10 minutes until golden. Leave to cool on the baking sheet.

Store the biscuits in an airtight tin and eat within 2 days.

BONUS POINT
• Toddlers grow at such a rate that snacks are vital to boost their nutritional needs. These savoury treats are a healthier option than sweet biscuits – especially if served with apple slices and a drink of milk.

OKAY FOR UNDER-ONES?
4–9 months Not suitable.
9–12 months Don't sprinkle the biscuits with sesame seeds before baking. Serve as finger food.

• Cut the dough into numerals, initials or animal shapes as you like.
• You can easily double the mixture and freeze some uncooked biscuits as a treat for another day. Cook from frozen, adding an extra few minutes to the cooking time.

PIZZA & SPINACH PALMIERS

These moreish cheesy pastries taste like pizza but they are made with ready-rolled puff pastry for convenience. **Makes 20**

425 g (14 oz) pack of 2 ready-rolled puff pastry sheets

4 tablespoons tomato ketchup

75 g (3 oz) frozen spinach, defrosted and well drained

125 g (4 oz) medium Cheddar cheese, grated

1 free-range egg, beaten

cherry tomatoes, to serve

Unroll one of the pastry sheets and spread with half of the tomato ketchup almost to the edges. Cover with half of the spinach and sprinkle with half of the cheese.

Brush the pastry edges with beaten egg, then roll the two opposite shorter sides of the pastry into the centre until they are touching.

Cut across the roll into thick slices and place cut-side up on lightly oiled baking sheets. If the palmiers are a little squashed, open them out with a small knife. Repeat with the other pastry sheet and remaining ingredients.

Brush the outside edges of the pastry with beaten egg. Bake in a preheated oven at 200°C (400°F) Gas Mark 6 for 10 minutes until well risen and golden.

Serve the palmiers warm on the day you make them, accompanied by cherry tomatoes.

BONUS POINTS
• This low salt, calcium-enriched savoury is a much healthier alternative than potato crisps or corn snacks.
• The spinach in these pastries is partly hidden – possibly just enough to cajole a child who would usually avoid it.

OKAY FOR UNDER-ONES?
4–9 months Not suitable.
9–12 months Offer a barely warm palmier broken into pieces.

• If you can't buy ready rolled pastry, use a 500 g (1 lb) pack chilled puff pastry. Halve and roll out each piece to a 28 x 23 cm (11 x 9 inch) rectangle.
• Vary the fillings: try finely chopped mushrooms in place of spinach; for simple palmiers, use only ketchup, cheese and a sprinkling of dried herbs; or for a vegan option, sprinkle with finely crumbled tofu instead of cheese.
• Encourage your child to help with spreading, rolling and brushing with egg, while you cut the palmiers and transfer them to the baking sheet.

MARBLED APRICOT & BANANA CAKE

This easy-to-make, moist banana cake is rippled with apricot purée and sandwiched together with a delicious cream cheese filling. **Serves 8**

250 g (8 oz) pack ready-to-eat dried
   apricots
200 ml (7 fl oz) apple juice or water
175 g (6 oz) soft margarine
100 g (3½ oz) caster sugar
2 small ripe bananas, 250 g (8 oz)
   unpeeled weight
200 g (7 oz) white self-raising flour
1 teaspoon baking powder
3 free-range eggs, beaten

Filling:
200 g (7 oz) low-fat cream cheese
2 tablespoons icing sugar
grated rind and juice of ½ orange

To finish:
icing sugar, for dusting

• For individual cakes, use two 12-hole bun trays lined with paper cases and cook for 12–15 minutes.
• Different dried fruits can be used for the purée, such as date or prune.
• Try using the fruit purée for the filling instead of the cream cheese.
• If your child is prone to asthma, buy dried apricots free from the preservative – sulphur dioxide – as this can trigger an asthma attack.

Lightly brush two 20 cm (8 inch) sandwich tins with oil and line the bases with greaseproof paper.

Put the apricots in a saucepan with the apple juice or water, cover and simmer gently for 10 minutes. Cool slightly, then purée the fruit with the juice in a food processor or blender until smooth. Set aside to cool.

Beat the margarine and sugar together until light and fluffy. Mash the bananas on a plate, then beat into the creamed mixture.

Sift the flour with the baking powder and gradually beat into the banana mixture, alternately with the beaten eggs.

Divide the cake mixture evenly between the tins, dot the apricot purée over the surface, then swirl a knife through the two mixtures to marble them.

Bake in a preheated oven at 180°C (350°F) Gas Mark 4 for about 20 minutes until well risen and golden, and the cakes spring back when pressed with a fingertip.

Leave in the tin for 15 minutes, then loosen the edges and turn out on to a wire rack. Peel off the lining paper and leave to cool completely.

For the filling, beat the cream cheese with the icing sugar, orange rind and juice. Use to sandwich the cooled cakes together.

Place the cake on a serving plate and dust with icing sugar to serve.

BONUS POINTS
• This cake contains much less sugar than a normal sandwich cake, because it derives sweetness from the bananas and apricots.
• Dried apricots are a good source of iron – essential for healthy blood cells – and potassium – needed to help regulate blood pressure and for the transmission of nerve impulses.
• Low-fat cream cheese contains much less fat and fewer calories than a more traditional buttercream filling, and is equally delicious.

OKAY FOR UNDER-ONES?
Not suitable, due to the sodium in self-raising flour and baking powder.

CRANBERRY & SUNFLOWER COOKIES

There is something irresistible about the wonderful aroma of freshly baked biscuits. Although they can be kept in an airtight tin for 2–3 days, most of these will disappear before they even have a chance to go cold! **Makes 25**

4 tablespoons sunflower seeds

2 tablespoons sunflower oil

75 g (3 oz) soft margarine

125 g (4 oz) light muscovado sugar

1 free-range egg

100 g (3½ oz) self-raising white flour

75 g (3 oz) self-raising wholemeal flour

grated rind of ½ small orange

75 g (3 oz) packet dried cranberries

Dry-fry the sunflower seeds in a nonstick frying pan, stirring constantly, for 2–3 minutes until golden. Grind to a fine paste with the oil, using a spice grinder, clean coffee grinder or pestle and mortar.

Cream the margarine and sugar together in a bowl (or food processor). Gradually beat in the egg, then mix in the flours. Mix in the sunflower paste, then stir in the orange rind and cranberries.

Drop heaped teaspoonfuls of the mixture on to lightly oiled baking sheets, spacing well apart. Bake in a preheated oven at 180°C (350°F) Gas Mark 4 for 10 minutes until golden. Leave on the baking sheets to firm up for a few minutes, then transfer to a wire rack to cool.

VARIATIONS

Triple chocolate cookies Omit sunflower seed paste, orange rind and cranberries. Use an extra 65 g (2½ oz) white self-raising flour and 15 g (½ oz) cocoa powder in place of the wholemeal flour. Stir in 75 g (3 oz) each dark and white chocolate dots at the end. Bake as above. (Illustrated above)

Sultana and orange cookies Use sultanas in place of the dried cranberries. (Illustrated above)

Apricot and cherry cookies Omit the cranberries and orange rind. Stir in 75 g (3 oz) each chopped ready-to-eat dried apricots and chopped natural, undyed glacé cherries.

BONUS POINT
• Unlike whole seeds, roasted and ground seeds can be given to children under 3. Sunflower seeds are a good source of protein and vitamin E; they are also high in linoleic acid – needed for the maintenance of cell membranes.

OKAY FOR UNDER-ONES?
Not suitable.

• Get your helper to measure out the ingredients, help with mixing and spoon the dough on to the baking sheets. Always supervise your child in the kitchen, and never let them open the oven door.

HELPING HANDS

You don't need a fancy cutter for these biscuits – just place your child's hands on a piece of card (or the back of a cereal packet), draw around them and cut out templates. Leave the decorations to your child's imagination. **Makes 20**

250 g (8 oz) plain flour

25 g (1 oz) cornflour

75 g (3 oz) caster sugar

few drops of vanilla essence

175 g (6 oz) unsalted butter, diced

a little caster sugar, for sprinkling

To decorate:

75 g (3 oz) good quality plain chocolate, in pieces

100 g (3½ oz) icing sugar, sifted

few ready-to-eat dried fruits, such as apricots and cranberries, and/or small sweets, such as Jelly Tots

Put the flour, cornflour and sugar into a bowl and add the vanilla essence. Add the butter and rub in using your fingertips (or a mixer) until evenly incorporated.

Bring the mixture together with your hands and knead gently to form a smooth dough. Roll out on a lightly floured surface with a floured rolling pin to a 5 mm (¼ inch) thickness. Cut out hand shapes from the dough, using card templates (see above) as a guide. Carefully lift the biscuits on to 2 baking sheets, using a palette knife. Gather the trimmings and re-roll to cut out more biscuits.

Sprinkle with a little extra sugar and bake in a preheated oven at 160°C (325°F) Gas Mark 3 for 10–12 minutes or until pale golden. Leave to cool on the baking sheets.

Melt the chocolate in a heatproof bowl over a pan of just boiled water. Stir until smooth. In a bowl, mix the icing sugar with 1 tablespoon water to a smooth thick paste.

Spoon the chocolate and icing into separate greaseproof paper piping bags and snip off the tips. Pipe on fingernails and decorations; add dried fruits and/or sweets as jewellery. Leave to harden for 1 hour. Eat on the same day (or store before icing in an airtight tin for 2–3 days).

VARIATIONS

Chocolate biscuits Replace half of the cornflour with 15 g (½ oz) sifted cocoa powder.

Spiced biscuits Add 1 teaspoon ground cinnamon in place of the vanilla essence, and use light muscovado instead of caster sugar.

OKAY FOR UNDER-ONES?

4–9 months Not suitable.

9–12 months Cut tiny shapes from the dough trimmings, bake without a sprinkling of sugar and serve as finger food. Ideally, under-ones shouldn't have foods with added sugar, but an occasional treat won't do any harm.

• Not all sweets are suitable for vegetarians. Some contain gelatine or animal derived colourings. See Food colourings (page 27).

ANIMAL MAGIC

Children enjoy making these as much as they love to eat them. Choose simple shaped animal cutters – those with tiny ears or tails can be difficult to fill and tricky to turn out. Encourage your child to identify the animal before he can take it off the plate! **Makes 16**

75 g (3 oz) butter or margarine

3 tablespoons golden syrup

200 g (7 oz) bar good quality plain chocolate, in pieces

100 g (3½ oz) Rice Krispies

50 g (2 oz) good quality white chocolate, in pieces

Brush 16 animal biscuit cutters with oil and place on a large oiled baking sheet.

Put the butter, syrup and plain chocolate in a saucepan and heat gently, stirring occasionally, until melted. Take off the heat and add the cereal, stirring to ensure it is well coated in chocolate.

Spoon the chocolate mixture into the animal cutters and press the mixture down well. Chill until firm.

Free the edges of the biscuits with a small knife or by flexing the cutters and remove.

Melt the white chocolate in a heatproof bowl over a pan of just boiled water, then spoon into a greaseproof paper piping bag and snip of the tip. Use to pipe features on to the animals and leave to harden for 30 minutes before serving.

BONUS POINT

• Breakfast cereal is fortified with iron and the B group of vitamins, of which vitamin B12 is the most difficult to obtain on a vegan diet.

OKAY FOR UNDER-ONES?

Not suitable.

• If you do not have enough animal cutters, spoon the remaining mixture into paper cases.

• For a simple alternative, make shape-sorter cakes. Press the chocolate mixture into an oiled 30 x 20 x 4 cm (12 x 8 x 1½ inch) loose-bottomed cake tin or foil-lined baking tin. Chill and cut into small squares, triangles or rounds. Serve in paper cake cases.

WE'VE GOT YOUR NUMBER

These little meringue numbers are easy to make, using a nylon piping bag and large plain tube. Even tiny children will be able to help squeeze the mixture out of the bag. **Makes 40**

2 free-range egg whites
100 g (3½ oz) caster sugar
few drops of food colouring (optional)

Line 2 baking sheets with nonstick baking paper. Whisk the egg whites in a large bowl until stiff, but not dry. Gradually whisk in the sugar, a teaspoonful at a time, and continue whisking until smooth and glossy.

Spoon half of the mixture into a nylon piping bag fitted with a large (no. 6) plain tube. Pipe numerals, about 7 cm (3 inches) high, on to one of the lined baking sheets. Colour the remaining meringue with a few drops of colouring, if required. Pipe coloured numbers on to the other baking sheet.

Bake in a preheated oven at 110°C (225°F) Gas Mark ¼ for 1¼–1½ hours or until the meringue numerals may be lifted off the paper easily. Leave to cool on the baking sheets.

Store the meringues in an airtight tin lined with greaseproof or nonstick baking paper for up to 4 days.

OKAY FOR UNDER-ONES?
Not suitable.

• Not all food colourings are suitable for vegetarians. Some are derived from animal sources – red colouring is often an offender. See food colourings (page 27).

• If you do not have a nylon piping bag and tube, make a large greaseproof paper piping bag and snip off the tip. Alternatively, use a strong polythene freezer bag with one of the corners snipped off. Or simply drop teaspoonfuls of meringue on to paper lined baking trays instead.

• Meringues may also be piped into letters of the alphabet, but be sure to make enough vowels for all the children to spell their own names!

Family meals

Food for all

Eating together as a family heralds a new stage in your baby's development – one that encourages social interaction as well as sharing the same food. These meals are adapted to suit a family with a young baby, an energetic toddler and parents who would like something more adventurous.

ROAST PUMPKIN & RISOTTO

Pumpkin is delicious roasted and served plain for children or sprinkled with chopped chilli and rosemary for adults; a mildly flavoured saffron risotto is the perfect complement. Butternut squash can be used instead of pumpkin.
Serves 2 adults, 1 toddler, and a baby over 4 months

750 g (1½ lb) pumpkin, deseeded and peeled

250 g (8 oz) risotto rice, rinsed

1 litre (1¾ pints) homemade vegetable stock (see page 38)

250 g (8 oz) shallots, halved if large

3 tablespoons olive oil

½–1 red chilli, deseeded and finely diced

2 fresh tender rosemary stems, chopped

large pinch of saffron strands

40 g (1½ oz) frozen peas or mixed vegetables

pinch of salt flakes and coarsely ground black pepper

rosemary sprigs, to garnish

• If your baby has a small appetite, keep half the purée for the next day.
• For older babies there is no need to sieve the purée.

For a baby, dice 100 g (3½ oz) pumpkin. Put into a small saucepan with 1 tablespoon rice and 150 ml (¼ pint) stock. Cover and simmer for 20 minutes until the rice is soft.

Thickly slice the remaining pumpkin. For toddler, put a few slices on a piece of foil, fold up the edges and place in a corner of a roasting tin. Scatter the remaining pumpkin and two-thirds of the shallots in the tin. Brush the vegetables with 2 tablespoons of the oil. Sprinkle the adult portions with chilli, rosemary and seasoning. Roast in a preheated oven at 200°C (400°F) Gas Mark 6 for 30 minutes until golden.

Meanwhile, finely chop the remaining shallots. Heat the remaining oil in a frying pan, add the shallots and fry until softened. Add the remaining rice and cook, stirring, for 1 minute. Add the saffron and half the stock. Simmer, stirring, for 20 minutes until creamy, topping up with extra stock as needed.

Purée the baby dinner, then press through a sieve. Cook the frozen vegetables in a small pan of boiling water for 3 minutes. Spoon the risotto on to a toddler plate and 2 adult plates. Chop the plain roasted pumpkin and add to the toddler plate, with peas or mixed vegetables. Add the rest of the pumpkin to the adult plates and garnish with rosemary to serve.

BONUS POINTS
• Pumpkin is easily digested and an ideal first food for babies. It is also a good source of beta-carotene and contains useful amounts of vitamin E.

MARINATED TOFU & STIR-FRIED VEGETABLES

Bright, colourful and packed with protein, vitamins and minerals – this meal looks as good as it tastes. **Serves 2 adults, 1 toddler, and a baby over 6 months**

285 g (9½ oz) pack chilled tofu, drained

4 teaspoons tomato ketchup

4 teaspoons soy sauce

6 teaspoons sunflower oil

2.5 cm (1 inch) piece of fresh root ginger, peeled and finely chopped

1 garlic clove, crushed

1 red pepper, halved, cored and deseeded

1 large courgette, about 200 g (8 oz)

75 g (3 oz) mangetout, halved lengthways

2 sheets dried egg noodles, about 250 g (8 oz)

3 spring onions, thickly sliced

2–3 tablespoons full-fat milk, soya milk or water

shredded spring onion, to garnish

• Soya is a common food allergen, so check with your health visitor before giving your baby tofu if there is a family history of food allergies.
• If you are planning to eat after rather than with the children, then marinate all of the tofu, but cook just enough noodles for your baby and toddler. Cook the noodles, stir-fry the vegetables and grill the tofu for your meal just before serving.

Set aside two thirds of the tofu for adults. Cut one-third off the other piece and reserve for the baby. Cut the rest of this smaller section into cubes for the toddler. Mix 2 teaspoons ketchup, 1 teaspoon soy sauce and 1 teaspoon oil in a small shallow dish, add the tofu cubes, toss together and set aside.

Cut the adult tofu into 2 pieces and score criss-cross lines on both sides. Mix the remaining ketchup and soy sauce with 2 teaspoons oil, the ginger and garlic in a large shallow dish. Add the scored tofu and brush with the marinade. Leave the toddler and adult tofu to marinate for 30 minutes.

For the baby, steam an eighth of the pepper and courgette for 4 minutes. Add 3 mangetout and steam for a further 2 minutes until tender. Set aside.

For the toddler, cut some pepper and courgette into thick strips; thread alternately on to 2 wooden skewers with the diced tofu. Place on a piece of foil on the grill rack. Lift the adult tofu portions on to a second piece of foil on the grill rack. Grill for 5 minutes until browned, turning once.

Meanwhile, cook the noodles in boiling water to packet directions.

Cut the remaining pepper and courgette into thin strips. Heat the remaining 3 teaspoons oil in a wok or frying pan, add the sliced pepper and courgette, mangetout and spring onions and stir-fry over a high heat for about 3 minutes. Drain the noodles and add to the stir-fry, keeping a few back for the baby; fry, stirring, for a further 30 seconds.

Purée the baby vegetables with the reserved noodles, plain tofu and milk or water to desired texture. Spoon into a baby bowl; check temperature before serving. Spoon some noodles on to the toddler plate and serve with the skewers.

Stir the reserved marinade into the stir-fry, then divide between adult plates and top with the tofu. Serve garnished with the spring onion if you like.

BONUS POINTS
• As fibre is removed during processing, tofu is very easy for babies to digest.
• Tofu is rich in protein, a good source of calcium and contains small amounts of vitamin E, phosphorus and iron. Tofu is also low in saturated fats.
• Suitable for a dairy-free diet if soya milk or water is used for baby meal.

RATATOUILLE WITH SPAGHETTI SQUASH

Spaghetti squash is often popular with young children. They are fascinated by the sight of it being teased into 'strands of spaghetti', as if by magic.
Serves 2 adults, 1 toddler, and a baby over 9 months

1 spaghetti squash
2 courgettes, about 425 g (14 oz), diced
1 red pepper, quartered, cored,
   deseeded and cut into strips
500 g (1 lb) plum tomatoes, skinned
2 tablespoons olive oil
1 onion, finely chopped
2 garlic cloves, crushed
2 tablespoons grated mild Cheddar
   cheese
1–2 tablespoons full-fat milk or water
25 g (1 oz) butter or margarine
salt and black pepper

To garnish:
few basil leaves
Parmesan cheese shavings
few marinated olives

• Spaghetti squash look rather like small oval yellow melons. If unobtainable, substitute 175 g (6 oz) dried spaghetti and cook in a saucepan of boiling water until just tender. Or use smaller pasta shapes if preferred.

Cut the squash in half crossways, then trim a thin slice off the bottom of each half to enable them to stand firmly. Scoop out the seeds from the centres. Place in a steamer over boiling water, cover and cook for 20 minutes.

Meanwhile, for a baby, set aside 100 g (3½ oz) courgette, ¼ red pepper and 1 tomato, discarding the seeds.

Heat 1 tablespoon oil in a saucepan. Add the onion and fry, stirring occasionally, until softened and lightly browned. Chop the rest of the tomatoes and add to the pan with the remaining courgettes, red pepper and half of the garlic. Cook uncovered, stirring occasionally, for 10 minutes until thickened.

Meanwhile, steam the baby's courgette and red pepper for 5 minutes. Lift the squash halves out of the steamer and tease the just cooked centres into strands with a fork. Put the baby's steamed vegetables, deseeded tomato, 75 g (3 oz) squash strands and 1 tablespoon grated Cheddar in a blender and blend with enough milk or water to give the desired texture; or finely chop the ingredients together.

Add the butter and 1 tablespoon oil to the remaining spaghetti squash strands and heat together.

For a toddler, shape a spaghetti squash nest in a shallow bowl, using a spoon and fork. Spoon some ratatouille around the edge and sprinkle with the rest of the grated Cheddar.

Add the remaining garlic and seasoning to the rest of the ratatouille and cook for 2 minutes. Spoon the spaghetti squash and ratatouille on to adult plates. Garnish with Parmesan shavings, basil leaves and olives to serve.

BONUS POINTS
• This recipe is ideal for anyone on a gluten-free diet.
• A suitable dish for vegans, if you omit the cheese and butter and use extra olive oil instead.

THAI-STYLE NOODLES

Nearly all children love pasta. For convenience, I have used thick rice noodles that simply require soaking in boiling water for this recipe. Mix and match the vegetables according to your family's preference or the dictates of the salad drawer. **Serves 2 adults, 1 toddler, and a baby over 6 months**

300 g (10 oz) rice noodles

2 carrots, about 200 g (7 oz), thinly sliced

150 g (5 oz) broccoli, cut into small
    florets, stems sliced

150 g (5 oz) cabbage, cored and finely
    shredded

150 ml (¼ pint) full-fat milk

2 tablespoons sunflower oil

75 g (3 oz) bean sprouts, well rinsed

1 tablespoon tomato ketchup

5 teaspoons soy sauce

1 teaspoon Thai green curry paste

2 garlic cloves, crushed

3 tablespoons chopped fresh coriander
    (optional)

3 eggs, beaten

shredded spring onion, to garnish

Put the noodles into a bowl and add boiling water to cover. Leave to soak for 3 minutes.

Meanwhile, for a baby's meal, put 25 g (1 oz) carrot, 25 g (1 oz) broccoli and 15 g (½ oz) cabbage into a small saucepan with the milk. Cover and simmer for 10 minutes.

Heat half the oil in a wok or large frying pan. Add the carrots and broccoli, toss to coat in the oil, then cover and cook over a moderate heat for 3 minutes, shaking the pan from time to time. Add the cabbage and stir-fry for 3 minutes.

Add 25 g (1 oz) noodles to the baby's vegetables and milk, then purée or finely chop to the desired texture.

Add the rest of the noodles to the stir-fry with the bean sprouts and cook for 1 minute, then stir in the tomato ketchup and 3 teaspoons of the soy sauce. Take out a portion for the toddler and set aside. Add the remaining soy sauce to the stir-fry with the curry paste, garlic and coriander, if using. Toss together and cook for 1 minute.

Heat the remaining oil in a large frying pan. Add the eggs and cook until set and golden brown underneath. Slide the omelette out on to a chopping board, roll up and cut into thin slices.

Spoon the stir-fry on to warmed plates for adults. Arrange egg strips on toddler and adult portions, and garnish the latter with shredded spring onion.

BONUS POINTS
• Rice noodles are suitable for those on a gluten-free diet.
• Cabbage and broccoli are both excellent sources of vitamin C. They also provide vitamin E, beta-carotene, folate, iron and potassium.

• Egg noodles may be substituted for the rice noodles, but do check the packet label – some contain sodium and should not be given to a child under 1 year.

CAULIFLOWER & LENTIL DHAL WITH TOMATOES

Dhal makes a great storecupboard supper, and you can easily vary the vegetables according to what you have in the vegetable rack or salad drawer of the fridge. Carrot and potato – and potato and frozen spinach – are good combinations. The dhal is mildly spiced for the children, while adult portions are spiked with chilli sauce and topped with crispy fried onions and tomatoes – speckled with fiery mustard seeds and cumin.
Serves 2 adults, 1 toddler, and a baby over 6 months

• Serve dhal with warmed naan bread or chapatis if liked. Okra is also a good accompaniment: trim, halve, rub with turmeric, cumin and paprika, then fry in a little oil with chopped garlic until tender.

175 g (6 oz) red lentils, rinsed
1 teaspoon turmeric
1 teaspoon finely ground cumin seeds
375 g (12 oz) cauliflower, cut into florets
400 g (13 oz) potatoes, diced
200 g (7 oz) basmati rice, rinsed
3 tomatoes, about 175 g (6 oz), skinned, deseeded and chopped
4 teaspoons sunflower oil
1 onion, thinly sliced
2 garlic cloves, sliced
1 teaspoon black mustard seeds
½ teaspoon cumin seeds, roughly crushed
3 tablespoons chopped fresh coriander (optional)
chilli sauce, to taste
salt and black pepper
coriander sprigs, to garnish

Put the lentils into a saucepan with 900 ml (1½ pints) water, the turmeric and ground cumin. Bring to the boil, lower the heat, cover the pan and simmer for 20 minutes until almost tender.

Add the cauliflower and potatoes to the pan, stir and top up with extra water if needed. Cover and simmer gently for 15 minutes.

Meanwhile, bring 450 ml (¾ pint) water to the boil in a separate pan. Add the rice, bring back to the boil and simmer, covered, for 10 minutes. Turn off the heat and leave to stand, covered, for 5 minutes.

For a baby, put 100 g (3½ oz) of the lentils and vegetables into a blender with 1 tablespoon rice, 1 tablespoon tomato and ½ teaspoon oil. Blend to the desired texture, adding a little extra water if needed.

Heat the remaining oil in a frying pan. Add the onion, garlic, mustard and cumin seeds and fry for 5 minutes until golden. Reserve a little tomato for the toddler; add the rest to the pan with the coriander, if using.

Spoon a little rice and dhal on to a plate for the toddler and top with the reserved raw tomato. Spoon the baby's food into a small bowl and check the temperature before serving.

Season the rest of the dhal well with salt and pepper, and flavour with chilli sauce to taste. Spoon the rice and dhal on to adult plates and top with the spiced onion and tomato mixture. Garnish with coriander to serve.

BONUS POINTS
• Combining lentils with rice supplies all of the essential amino acids to provide complete protein.
• The tomato garnish adds vitamin C and helps the body's absorption of iron from the lentils.

CHESTNUT SOFRITO

This aromatic casserole of chickpeas, chestnuts, carrots and sweet potato has a Middle Eastern flavour. Couscous with a hint of orange – and flecked with fragrant mint and parsley for the adults – is the ideal complement.
Serves 2 adults, 1 toddler, and a baby over 9 months

1 tablespoon olive oil

1 onion, finely chopped

2 garlic cloves, crushed

2.5 cm (1 inch) piece fresh root ginger, peeled and finely chopped

1 sweet potato, about 200 g (7 oz), halved lengthways and thickly sliced

2 carrots, about 200 g (7 oz), diced

400 g (13 oz) can chopped tomatoes

450 ml (¾ pint) homemade vegetable stock (see page 38)

250 g (8 oz) can whole chestnuts, drained

400 g (13 oz) can chickpeas, drained and rinsed

½ teaspoon turmeric

1 cinnamon stick, halved

salt and black pepper

To serve:

175 g (6 oz) couscous

100 g (3½ oz) green beans

juice of 1 orange

4 tablespoons chopped mixed fresh parsley and mint (or just parsley)

• If allergy is a consideration, omit the canned chestnuts and add an extra sweet potato instead.
• For 5–9 month babies, serve sweet potato and carrot purée on its own.

Heat the oil in a saucepan, add the onion and fry for 5 minutes until softened and pale golden. Stir in the garlic and ginger and cook for a further 2 minutes.

For a baby, put 25 g (1 oz) sweet potato and 50 g (2 oz) carrot into a small saucepan with 1 tablespoon tomato juice (from the can) and 150 ml (¼ pint) stock. Cover and simmer for 15 minutes or until tender.

Meanwhile, add the remaining sweet potato, carrots, tomatoes and stock to the onions, with the chestnuts and chickpeas. Bring to the boil, stirring. For a toddler, transfer two ladlefuls to an individual casserole dish. Add the turmeric, cinnamon and seasoning to the rest of the sofrito, then transfer to a medium-small casserole.

Cover both dishes and cook in a preheated oven at 180°C (350°F) Gas Mark 4 for 1 hour until tender.

Blend the baby's vegetables with some of the cooking liquid to give the desired texture; or chop finely if preferred. Cover and refrigerate until needed.

Shortly before serving, put the couscous in a bowl, pour on 450 ml (¾ pint) boiling water and leave to soak for 5 minutes. Cook the green beans in boiling water for 5 minutes, then drain. Drain any excess water from the couscous and stir in the orange juice, using a fork.

Spoon a little couscous into the baby's dish. Reheat the baby's vegetable mixture until piping hot, then cool to serving temperature. Add to the baby's couscous and serve with a few green beans for finger food.

Spoon some couscous into the toddler's dish and top with the toddler casserole. Chop some green beans and sprinkle over the top.

Add the herbs to the remaining couscous and season with salt and pepper to taste. Spoon on to adult plates, top with sofrito and serve with the rest of the beans.

BONUS POINTS
• Mixing nuts with pulses makes this a high protein meal, but do make sure that you buy canned chestnuts and chickpeas without sugar or salt.
• Adding fresh orange juice to the soaked couscous helps to boost vitamin C levels and is particularly useful for children who are reluctant fruit eaters.

VEGETABLE QUARTET WITH PARSNIP MASH

A medley of green vegetables tossed in a lemon and tomato dressing – served with a smooth, creamy parsnip mash – makes a quick and easy midweek supper. For your toddler, the mash is enriched with toasted seed butter for added protein, and served with plain steamed green vegetables. For your baby, there is a simple mixed vegetable purée.

Serves 2 adults, 1 toddler, and a baby over 5 months

750 g (1½ lb) parsnips, halved and cored

3 baby leeks, about 75 g (3 oz), well washed and thickly sliced

100 g (3½ oz) green beans, halved

150 g (5 oz) frozen baby broad beans

125 g (4 oz) broccoli, cut into florets

4 teaspoons olive oil

2 tablespoons pumpkin seeds

2 tablespoons sesame seeds

4 tablespoons full-fat milk

2–3 tablespoons formula milk, home-made stock (see page 38) or water

25 g (1 oz) butter

4 tablespoons fromage frais

a little tomato ketchup (optional)

2 teaspoons sun-dried tomato paste

juice of ½ lemon

salt and black pepper (optional)

• From 6–9 months, cow's milk and fromage frais can be added to the baby's vegetable purée.

• From 9–12 months, add a few broad beans, plus 1–2 teaspoons of the seed paste. Coarsely purée or mash according to baby's stage.

Cut the parsnips into chunks and cook in boiling water in the base of a steamer for 10 minutes. Put the other vegetables in the top of the steamer, cover and cook for 5 minutes until just tender.

Meanwhile, heat 1 teaspoon olive oil in a frying pan, add the pumpkin and sesame seeds and fry until golden. Grind 1 tablespoon of the seed mixture with 1 tablespoon full-fat milk to a smooth paste; set aside for the toddler's meal.

Take the steamer off the pan, drain the parsnips thoroughly, then mash smoothly.

For a baby, blend 2 tablespoons of the mash with 2 green beans, 2 broccoli florets and enough formula milk, stock or water to give the desired texture. Spoon into a baby dish.

Add the butter, fromage frais and remaining full-fat milk to the parsnip mash and mix well.

For a toddler, spoon a portion of mash on to a plate and mix in the ground seeds. Add a portion of vegetables, plus a little ketchup if required.

For adults, toss the rest of the green vegetables with the sun-dried tomato paste, the remaining olive oil, lemon juice and salt and pepper to taste. Spoon on to warmed plates, add the parsnip mash and sprinkle with the toasted seeds to serve.

BONUS POINTS

• Serve your toddler's meal with a drink of fresh orange juice, diluted half and half with water, or follow with a piece of fresh fruit, for a well-balanced meal with plenty of vitamin C.

• Seeds provide a good source of protein. Eating them in combination with other protein foods – such as the broad beans and fromage frais – boosts levels of essential amino acids.

SMOKY JOES

Toddlers love the informality of this kind of food – which even mum and dad eat with their fingers! Grilling the aubergine slowly gives it the most wonderful smoky flavour, though you can achieve the same effect on the barbecue or by holding it directly over a burner on a gas hob if preferred.
Serves 2 adults, 1 toddler, and a baby over 9 months

2 small aubergines, about 500 g (1 lb)

2 tablespoons olive oil

2 small courgettes, about 300 g (10 oz), cut into sticks

1 onion, finely chopped

1 garlic clove, crushed

200 g (7 oz) can baked beans

6 small flour tortillas

1 Little Gem lettuce, shredded

1 tablespoon grated mild Cheddar cheese

210 g (7½ oz) can red kidney beans

1 teaspoon hot chilli sauce, or to taste

3 tablespoons chopped fresh coriander

salt and black pepper

To garnish:

lime wedges

coriander sprigs

Pierce the stalk end of the aubergines with a fork. Place on the grill rack and grill for 30 minutes, turning several times, until the skin is blackened and charred all over. Cool slightly, then peel off the skin. Chop the aubergine flesh and set aside.

Heat 1 tablespoon of the oil in a frying pan, add the courgette sticks and fry for 5 minutes until tender. Lift out of the pan with a slotted spoon.

Heat the remaining oil in the pan, add the onion and garlic, and fry for 5 minutes until softened. Add the aubergine and heat through.

Warm the baked beans in a small saucepan for the baby and toddler. Warm the tortillas according to pack directions.

For a toddler, put one tortilla on a plate, add a little lettuce, a spoonful of the aubergine mixture, a few courgette sticks and two spoonfuls of baked beans. Roll up, so your toddler can pick it up to eat.

For a baby, mash 2–3 tablespoons baked beans and place in a bowl. Sprinkle with the cheese and serve with strips of tortilla as finger food.

Drain the red kidney beans and add to the aubergine mixture with the chilli sauce and chopped coriander. Heat through and season with salt and pepper to taste.

Spoon the shredded lettuce, aubergine mixture and courgette sticks on to adult tortillas. Roll up and serve two each, garnished with lime wedges and coriander sprigs.

BONUS POINTS
• Serving pulses, such as kidney beans and baked beans, with grain foods such as tortillas, boosts protein levels.
• Courgettes are a useful source of beta-carotene, vitamin C and folate.

• Buy baked beans without added salt and sugar, or at least opt for a low-salt, low-sugar brand. Offer in small amounts to begin with, as beans are high in fibre.

• Try offering your baby a little finely chopped or mashed aubergine mixed with 1–2 tablespoons fromage frais or natural bio yogurt.